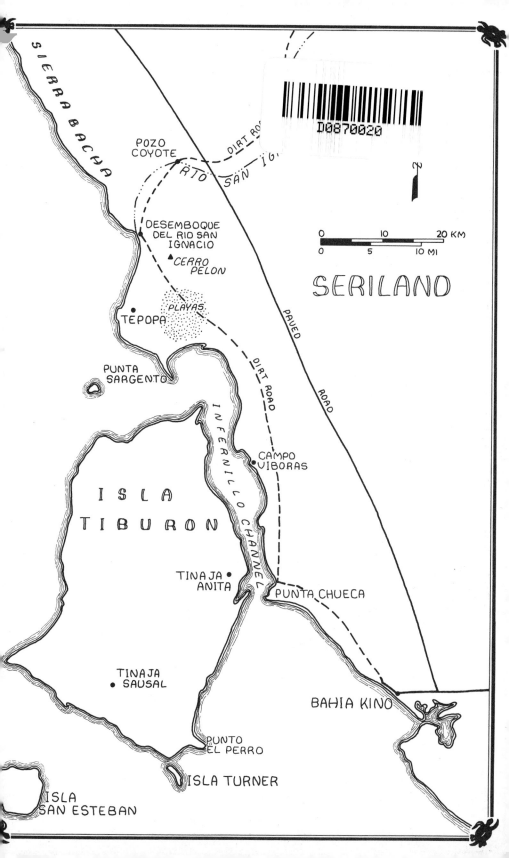

SIERRA BACHA

POZO
COYOTE

DIRT ROAD

RIO SAN IG.

DESEMBOQUE
DEL RIO SAN
IGNACIO

▲ CERRO
PELON

PLAYAS

TEPOPA

PUNTA
SARGENTO

SERILAND

0   10   20 KM
0   5   10 MI

PAVED ROAD

DIRT ROAD

INFERNILLO CHANNEL

CAMPO
VIBORAS

ISLA
TIBURON

TINAJA
ANITA

PUNTA CHUECA

TINAJA
SAUSAL

BAHIA KINO

PUNTO
EL PERRO

ISLA TURNER

ISLA
SAN ESTEBAN

Where the Desert
Meets the Sea

Where the Desert Meets the Sea

A Trader in the Land of the Seri Indians

David Yetman

Black and white photographs by Jim Hills

PEPPER PUBLISHING
A Division of Arran Enterprises, Ltd.

Maps and tone of line drawings of Seri carvings, baskets and necklaces by Chris Sternberg

Library of Congress Cataloging-in-Publication Data

Yetman, David, 1941-
  Where the desert meets the sea.

  1. Seri Indians—Social life and customs.
  2. Indians of Mexico—Sonora (State)—Social life and customs.
  3. Yetman, David, 1941   . I. Title.
  F1221.S43Y48 1988   972'.1700497   87-29242
  ISBN 0-914468-26-X

Published by PEPPER PUBLISHING
        433 North Tucson Boulevard
        Tucson, AZ 85716-4744
Printed in the United States of America

First Edition

International Standard Book Number 0-914468-26-X   Clothbound
International Standard Book Number 0-914468-28-6   Paperback
Library of Congress Catalogue Card Number 88-060121

Contents

Acknowledgements

Numerous individuals assisted me in the preparation of this book. Jim Hills, with whom I have traveled, traded and talked for thirty years, made many suggestions, including the chapter on dogs. Scott Ryerson, a Seri trader who reviewed the manuscript, made many important critical remarks. Dr. Richard Felger brought to my attention numerous facts I had forgotten or overlooked. My wife, Lynn Fowler, made many valuable suggestions, as did Peggy Lockard, who, as my editor and publisher, was most patient and understanding in getting the manuscript into publishable form. My son, Chris, made observations that improved the prose.

Friends who reviewed the manuscript at various stages include: Pat Conlee, Nancy Ames, Monica Carillo, Conrad Joyner, Carl Noggle and Corky Poster.

Most important were the Seris themselves, especially Santiago Astorga, as dear and fine a man as exists anywhere, José Astorga, Amalia Astorga, Chapo Barnet, Adolfo Burgos, Roberto Campuzano, Roberto Herrera, Angelita Torres and the late Fernando Romero. With them I have had countless hours of conversation and have learned much of the Seri Way.

Preface

Only yesterday it was an immense desert, unconquered by machines. Now a highway has tamed the desert's arrogant vastness. If you drive west on it, fast from the teeming, dusty streets of Hermosillo, you will speed past uniform, spiritless fields of crops tended by obedient robot machines, past factories of listless, mechanized hens in tenements where the lights are never dimmed and through vast croplands where once flowed the waters of the late Río Sonora. Hurrying toward the setting sun, you will pass through settlements where the poor—defiant of dust and death—wait in tar paper huts for jobs that seldom come. Pressing north a hundred miles, you follow a nearly deserted road that points toward the monster power plant at Puerto Libertad. If your car is big and powerful, the air conditioner will deny the desert heat, obscure the misery of the field laborers and conceal the dust of once green fields abandoned to their fate, where the desert slowly reclaims itself. Tune in your stereo, loud, for only so will you blot out the silence of the pitiless landscape.

Don't leave the road. For the unaware, there is no safety away from the black ribbon laid down by men and their machines. The desert is a perpetual reminder of what men choose to deny. Its vastness, its blank, relentless drought do not argue, they merely underscore, merely assert its finality. To struggle against it is futile. Already the highway, but a few years old, recedes against the onslaught of the desert. Desert plants force the pavement to buckle and flash floods undercut the pavement, taking huge bites from the road.

But I will reveal to you a secret. Exactly 100 kilometers north of the last gas pump on the highway to Puerto Libertad, beyond all the vineyards and the fields of wheat and cotton, beyond the brandy stills and the billboards proclaiming pesticides, there is a farm—an *ejido*—where only a decade ago reeled the shadows of indignant desert birds. A few huts, a couple of fields; vainly, pathetically feigning abundance, the farm is little more than a temporary incursion into the desert's domain.

When you see the tiny sign "San Ignacio" drive west and south, away from the security of the asphalt on to dirt; drive across the fields of the fading farm, past an ancient ranch, by a windmill, around a corral, down a draw, across a dry wash, through a forest of mesquite, ironwood, palo verde, cardón and organ pipe. Drive on, slowly now, for the road is sandy and washboard.

The road leaves the draw. Soon you ascend a small hill and from a side of the gentle rise you behold one of the fairest sights in all of God's creation. There, towards the setting sun, across a shimmering desert plain, lies the sparkling Sea of Cortez.

Look to the south. Before you are hard mountains of solid rock with caves wherein dwell, some say, vague unknown spirits. Beware of them, ancient forces all, for those who have beheld them warn that the spirits of the caves possess the beholder with a vision, with a hypnotic quest that cannot be evaded.

Look to the north. Here are steep, dry, rocky hills that reach to the edge of the sea. Enter there with caution, for the way is guarded by *cirios*, the boojum trees, the only survivors, so goes the myth, of a race of once-powerful giants who ruled the earth. To this day they retain their power, ready to unleash awful and destructive winds at any insolence, and visit the unsuspecting with calamity.

Look west again, toward the sea. Don't be deceived by the wild beauty. It is a brutal land where the sun daily creates and destroys, where the winter winds blow without mercy, where the rains tease with a whore's promise, and where the sun sucks life's moisture from the unknowing. Here, of those who are ignorant, the weak will die quickly, perhaps a blessing, for the strong face a more agonizing demise. Only those who have learned the desert's secrets can hope to survive.

Stay and watch the sun till the day fades in the haze of the sea. Then drive, quickly now, lurching, then swaying over the sand and washboard, a league to the west, through the ruts and dust and junk, to a village of stern cottages thrown upon the earth like a dimestore Stonehenge.

Drive through the village until you reach the sandy shore, till you smell ironwood smoke and hear the sound of machetes whittling the dense grain of the ironwood tree, mingled with the music of children's voices and the waves of the sea. Listen and smell.

Stop now, for you can go no farther. Stop. Leave your car behind and walk to the sea. Listen as they approach, sometimes silently, sometimes with the sound of summer heat, sometimes with voices speaking a musical language unknown to the children of Columbus. But always they come. Soon they are upon you. They are gentle, they are curious. Women they are, breathing a strange and wonderful tongue. They may touch your car and admire your clothes or inspect your light hair and pale skin, but they will not harm you.

They are the People, the Seris. They have been here since the written word appeared in the New World and will be here until the desert and sea die. Watch them. Follow them, for they have much to teach. If some day, far in the mists of the ages you hear they are gone, you will know the end of the world cannot be far behind. And if, some day, wearied and disillusioned with the smudge and toil of men's machines you must find the world as it was, come back, back to where the desert meets the sea. If the People are here still, then hope remains.

Campuzano's Boat

It was a brisk spring morning at the northern end of the Infernillo (Little Hell) Channel. The early fog had burned off and the air was sharp and clear, the brownish gray of the rugged mountains contrasting with the deep blue water of the Gulf of California. The Seri boat, an insignificant dot in the Sea of Cortez, churned against the tidal current that flowed south to north. I rode in the bow of the small plank craft, shivering from the chilling spray as we rounded Tepopa point heading south.

From my vantage point I could see most of the Seri country, a land of little rain where the sun relentlessly bakes the parched earth. Far to the northwest I could make out the outline of Isla Angel de la Guarda (Guardian Angel Island) and, behind it, the promontories of Baja California, more than sixty miles away. To the east, the stark plains stretched into the coastal hills. To the west lay the northern end of Isla Tiburón (Shark Island), desert paradise, wildlife sanctuary and former home of many of the Seri Indians.

The rocky, barren slopes of this empty land are strangers to the rains that smooth out the hills of more temperate climates. Still, the desert defies the drought by producing magnificent stands of organ pipe and the giant cardon cacti, elephant trees and numerous shrubs and grasses. And this year in particular, the sparse rains had fallen at the right moment, producing a carpet of flowers.

Roberto Campuzano and Aurora Astorga

At the motor was Roberto Campuzano, a tall, stately Seri man of thirty-five. Father of a son and four daughters, Campuzano was one of a diminishing number of younger Seri men who kept their hair in a long double braid and still wore the traditional male loincloth over their trousers. His jet-black hair, lovingly braided by his wife Aurora Astorga, trailed behind his head from time to time as the sea breeze caught us.

Campuzano, a proud, traditional Seri, was widely acknowledged to be one of the best boatmen and fishermen among the Seris, a fact that reassured me in the deep, choppy seas at Tepopa's foot. We wore no life jackets. Capitán, his seven year-old son, dragged a fishing line in the water, leaning over the side of the boat to see where his lure was trailing. Campuzano watched him with pride and confidence.

Almost two thousand feet above us Tepopa was still shrouded in fog. Campuzano called and motioned to me to look up toward the peak. There, on a rim overlooking the water, two desert bighorn sheep were copulating, a scene which gave rise to considerable laughter and discussion among the three Seri men in the boat. Lacking fluency in the Seri language I could only surmise the content of their remarks.

We had left Desemboque at sunrise that March morning in 1971, heading for Kino Bay, almost seventy miles to the south. En route we would stop at Isla Tiburón, Campo Viboras, an important Seri camp, and Punta Chueca.

As people of the sea, Seris love boat rides. Many present members were alive when the tribe was still semi-nomadic, and in conversation with me they express nostalgia for those days. Until the 1970s most families spent part of the year in the permanent villages of Desemboque or Punta Chueca and part in camps near Kino Bay or Puerto Libertad, now the site of a huge power generating plant and a city of about 4,000 souls. Or they would spend a few weeks in smaller Seri settlements such as Campo Almond, Campo Paredones, Campo Sarjento or Campo Víboras, all located at the very edge of the water. Their peregrinations were determined by the abundance of fish and sea life at various camps.

In the summer all would spend as much time as possible in Punta Chueca or in Desemboque, Campuzano's home, because only in this site is there freedom from *jejenes*, biting gnats that descend on human victims like invisible vampires, worse than the legendary black flies of the frozen north. Jejenes can turn life into a tormented, itching hell. Since they breed in mangrove estuaries, areas adjacent to such swamps have to be avoided during summer months. Jejenes are less a problem in Punta Chueca, in spite of its adjacent mangroves, because it is blessed with breezes that tend to blow the miserable creatures away.

Fortunately for the Seris, their boats gave them the mobility they needed to survive and escape the fiery onslaughts of the jejenes. The boats came to symbolize freedom, as well as provide the means to freedom. Today pickup trucks also symbolize freedom now that the Seris' art work and reliance on Mexican stores have made them less mobile. Even now young people will wade out to the boats in the evenings and take a spin around the bay, generally with the excuse that they are fishing, but in reality, I think, just to have the pleasure of being in a boat in the water.

As I looked back inside the boat I could see signs of the old mobility. On the spur of the moment Campuzano had decided to take off for a couple of days and had, in five minutes, packed provisions for himself and his two young sons and hopped into the boat. In those days, it was not at all unusual to be visiting with a family one evening and find them gone in the morning, having thrown their few possessions and dogs and cats into the family boat and headed to their favorite spot for a month or so. A year ago I had come to Desemboque looking for Campuzano, only to learn that he and his family had just departed for Puerto Libertad, forty miles to the north to spend part of the winter.

This mobility could be hard on traders like me. On one evening I advanced a Seri 200 pesos ($16) for an ironwood carving only to find the next morning that he and his clan had departed for more comfortable surroundings. When they returned many weeks later, he had "forgotten" the advance.

These meanderings were not without peril. Surprisingly, few Seris swim well, most not at all. Back in the 1950s an entire family, save one, was lost—ten people in all—when their boat capsized in heavy seas en route from Desemboque to Puerto Libertad. The women, with their massive skirts and children clinging to them, were helpless and drowned immediately. The men trying to save them fared no better. The loss of the family was a terrible blow to the Seris.

Now, with mobility stifled by economic necessity, the boats are an artifact connecting the Seris to their past, a link between them and nature. Although the boats may have lost much of their practical importance, they remain a reminder of a time lost to them, when only the sea stood between them and another home.

But I was aboard Campuzano's panga at a time when boats were more integrated into Seri life, and I was happy on this particular morning to be in the relative safety of the Infernillo. The Infernillo is a picturesque channel passing between two parallel ranges of desert mountains. Deep enough under most circumstances for large shrimp boats to pass through, its currents can be deceptive. The channel varies from about two miles wide at the southern end near Santa Rosa to about six miles wide near Punto Sarjento in the north.

Seri boatmen know every inch of the thirty-mile long channel and of these boatmen, Campuzano rated with the best. This was another reason why I felt comfortable riding with him. Seri boats were clumsy, heavy things in those days and hydrodynamically primitive, an uneasy marriage of modern technology and archaic function. Made entirely of wood with ribs of dense mesquite and planking of rough pine, they easily weighed a ton. But

Campuzano could maneuver his boat with consummate skill. As long as the motor did not fail (the Seri's abilities as mechanics do not match their expertise as fishermen) I was content. It was a good time I reckoned, to be on this boat, among friends and to be part of the life of the Seris in one of the most wildly beautiful areas on earth.

The motor droned on and suddenly the boat appeared to flounder. I looked with concern at Campuzano, mindful of the stories of drownings I had heard. As usual, his face showed little emotion, but he gave me a hint of a smile. Santiago Astorga, Campuzano's brother-in-law, a dear, sensitive friend and deep thinker, reassured me that the tide was changing. Protected from the heavy seas by Isla Tiburón on the west and the mainland on the east, the Infernillo has numerous currents but few waves, which the boatman fears most. Now the current would move from north to south, helping us along. It was that sudden. Ramón Lopez, a dour, talented artist not prone to conversation, who, along with his two young sons and Capitán, comprised the rest of the boat's passengers, paid little heed.

As I looked backward, I could see a one-foot high tidal bore bearing down on us from a couple of hundred yards away. Just before it reached us the water became so shallow I saw sand dollars on the channel bottom. There couldn't have been more than a couple of feet of water remaining beneath us. The bore struck, lifting us. The motor surged, labored, then as the small wave passed, resumed its normal monotonous hum. Campuzano gave no indication that anything had happened. He had been swept along with tidal bores hundreds of times before.

Seri boatmen take their position as captain very seriously. Campuzano, very much in charge, looked so stately any utterance would have detracted from his august appearance. Truly competent in everything he undertook, there was no question that he was master, that he had sung the appropriate song to control the winds before we embarked. Yet the dreamy look in his face showed he was not immune to the primitive beauty that surrounded us.

We headed for an ancient Seri encampment on Isla Tiburón and beached there. No one explained why the stop was made, but I surmised that its purpose was a renewal, a token stop to remind the men this was where their roots were, this was their real home.

While on the island, little Capitán was quiet and, I thought, rather reverent. We walked around the remains of countless years of ocotillo and brush huts. We found the bones of many schools of fish cast there by ancestors lost to time, to be preserved almost forever by the pristine dryness of the Gulf coast.

I was struck by the quiet power of the place. A flood of images came to mind: a hardy, untamed people surviving centuries in a land where the intensity of the climate has claimed many lives; a tribe whose survival was dependent upon their ability to extract from a recalcitrant nature the means of survival in a way the technologically sophisticated may never understand; a tribe who had to overcome the threat of extinction first by Spaniards, later by Mexicans, and later yet by poverty and disease, by managing to sustain life from the reluctant desert where less hardy souls feared to tread.

We spoke no words while on the island. I had numerous questions but held my tongue when I noted the Seris were themselves silent. As most who know the Seris intimately will relate, when in their own element they often possess an intimidating spiritual power. I was also very much in their physical power. They had control over the boat which would deliver me, in a few hours, to Kino Bay. From there I would hurry home to resume my duties as a philosophy professor at Arizona State University.

Campuzano now headed the boat eastward across the Infernillo to Campo Víboras where we stayed for a few minutes, exchanging pleasantries with the four or five families who would dwell there until the jejenes returned in the warm months. Santiago left an amorphous bundle of something with one of the families. I shook hands with them and then we were off to Punta Chueca, greeted every few minutes by a group of dolphins who leaped from the water, apparently assuring us the passage would be safe and maybe hoping someone would stop and play for a while.

I understand why the Seris chose Punta Chueca as a principal village. Situated on a small peninsula, its tiny harbor is almost always protected from the prevailing northwesterly winds and although it is close to mangrove estuaries, the breezes keep most of the jejenes away. It is only twenty land miles and little farther by water from Kino Bay, its shops, modern conveniences and the hordes of tourists who have brought prosperity (and rapid cultural change) to the Seris.

I also suspect that the hundred or so permanent or intermittently nomadic Seri residents stayed there because of the closeness of the sea and Isla Tiburón. A Seri can hop into a boat and scud across the Infernillo to Tiburón and its permanent spring located only a few miles inland in fifteen minutes, a vast improvement over the hour or so journey from Desemboque to the island.

We stopped only briefly at Punta Chueca, whose inhabitants seem much more affected by Mexican and North American influences than those from Desemboque, which is more purely Seri. Although all Seris have relatives in both villages, the Astorgas (with whom I had become quite close) and Roberto Campuzano have long had their roots in Desemboque and are regarded as Desemboqueñans. Some of the people of Punta Chueca, partially because he is a man of action and a producer who doesn't waste time, regard Campuzano as aloof and proud, and consequently we spent little time exchanging information. There appeared to be little interaction of my Seri friends with the residents of Punta Chueca.

Still, the typical crowd had gathered around the boat as it beached and a few women tried halfheartedly to sell me ironwood carvings. My friends went off to Alfredo Topete's general store to buy soda pop while I hung around the boat, nervous lest we be too long delayed and I miss my bus in Kino.

But Campuzano did not seem inclined to tarry either. Soon we were back in the boat with only a few wistful goodbyes from vendors whose art I had not been willing to purchase. An hour later we reached the long white beach of Kino Bay. Campuzano headed directly for the nearest sandy area and buried the prow in the sand.

We wasted no time getting out. A group of North American tourists stared curiously as a Seri boat filled with wild-looking Indians coughed up a blond professor with suitcase in hand. Ramón and his sons disembarked with me intending to accompany me to Hermosillo to visit a doctor.

I paid Campuzano for the boat trip (Seris do *nothing* for free) and shook hands with him and Santiago. Then, without a word, they pushed the boat out, jumped in, started the motor and headed back north. Their mission was over. They had returned a wayward gringo to civilization.

We had only a brief wait before the old rattletrap bus that lumbered between Hermosillo and Kino Bay drove up. I climbed the steps, paid my fare and settled down in a seat, my suitcase full of carvings next to me. Ramón and his sons sat several seats away from me. Not a friendly guy, I thought. But then he probably thought me extravagant with emotions, a typical gringo.

As we waited for the driver I reflected on Ramón's behavior. Was he just more direct with the other Seris? When the chips were down would any of them regard me as a true friend? Or was the warmth I felt for them a one-sided emotion, their acceptance of me more a tolerance than a real liking? As a trader I brought useful consumer goods and a lot of money to the villagers and in buying and selling I came to know many of them well. But for my own self-esteem I hoped they didn't like me, well, just for my money. Later on I was to learn that they treat everyone, even each other, with aloofness.

The bus driver climbed aboard, started the noisy engine and slammed the ancient bus into gear. I looked over the broad sweep of Kino Bay, overcome with the immensity and isolation of Isla Tiburón far in the distance, and of the Seri country looming, beckoning to the north.

Someday, I vowed, I would come back and never leave.

Comcaac

Although I haven't gone back for good, I have not been able to stay away. As the years have passed I have seen vast, culturally devastating changes come to the Seris, or Comcaac as they call themselves. The changes in their way of life have had a deep affect on me also. Part of the changes they have experienced, although only a small part, are, for better or worse, a result of my contact with them. This book is about the Seris as I saw them.

After I first visited the Seri lands in 1968 I began to import their ironwood carvings and market them in Tucson. I was joined in this effort by Hugh Holub, later to become a Tucson attorney, who was instrumental in publicizing the sculptures. Together we tried, with some success, to bring to the attention of Indian art lovers the extraordinary achievements of Seri sculptors.

Over the next five years I made dozens of trips to the Seri country and developed a fascination and respect for the Seri people. These remarkable Indians live on the arid northwest coast of the Mexican state of Sonora in an area of several hundred square miles which they hold as ejidos, or communal property under title from the Mexican government.

Until the middle part of this century their favored residence was on Isla Tiburón in the Gulf of California, a massive island with considerable game and a dependable inland water supply. Always nomadic, they had roamed for centuries over a much larger domain extending from Guaymas in the south to as far north as Puerto Lobos, and considerably inland. The Seris resisted attempts by Jesuits and later by Franciscans to incorporate them into agricultural life around missions, doggedly refusing to give up their nomadic tendencies. Persecution by Spaniards and later by Mexicans forced them to reside exclusively on the hot, desert coast of Sonora, a land thought to be of little value for agriculture, mining or ranching and thence onto Isla Tiburón.

After facing near extinction in the last century, their numbers were still dwindling in the 1940s but are increasing today. Due to intermarriage with Mexicans it is hard to determine precisely how many Seris exist, but about 550 people speak the Seri language as a first language, live in Seri lands and are considered Seri by other Seris.

Because their environment is characterized by sparse rainfall, less than four inches per year, and summer temperatures in excess of 100 degrees, their lands have never been able to support a large population, nor is agriculture possible without technical sophistication and heavy capital investment, both unavailable to the Seris. Irrigated lands to the east and north face drastic declines in productivity because of dwindling water supplies and salinization of the soil, so an agricultural future is still improbable. Even if agricultural resources were available, I don't think the cultural values still heavily imbued in the Seris would make them successful farmers. Attempts by missionaries, after the Spanish conquest, to make the Seris tillers of the soil, failed miserably. I doubt they would be much more successful now.

Climatic extremes isolate them from their other neighbors: Tohono O'odham (Papago) live 100 miles to the north; Yaquis and Mayos live 100 miles to the south and Pima Bajos 150 miles to the east. Opatas, with whom the Seris had some contact, are either extinct or completely assimilated into Mexican society. Contact with the other tribes has taken place, but only minimally. They speak admiringly of Apaches, but few have ever seen any.

Of the Seris, more than any other indigenous people of northwest Mexico, it can be said that there is a mystique—whether due to their hardiness, their wild appearance, their primitive living conditions or their occasional desperation for water. Following some of their early encounters with Mexicans and North Americans, stories were circulated that the Seris were cannibals, a preposterous myth the Seris sometimes find amusing, sometimes infuriating. The myth has been so widely circulated that the Seris have, justifiably, felt looked down upon by the dominant Mexican culture. A Seri once showed me an article from a Mexican tabloid that related stories of cannibalism among Seris. Knowing that the stories were utterly false, I was amused. The Seri was not.

There is little question that they took advantage of the first cattle appearing on their lands, a new source of food with a superb flavor and easy to come by. Some battles ensued in the mid-1800s in which the Encinas family, owners of the cattle, enlisted the cooperation of the Mexican government to drive the Seris out of much of their former lands and onto Isla Tiburón and a narrow strip of land along the coast where cattle found little to graze upon. The desire of Mexicans to eject the Seris from their land may explain the origin of the myth of cannibalism, providing the government with an easy rational for a policy of benevolent extermination. Mexico's treatment of Indians inhabiting lands coveted by settlers closely paralleled similar treatment of Indians by the U.S. government. They were forced to endure horrible suffering at the hands of their persecutors.

In contrast with many other Indian groups and perhaps owing to the abundance of seafood in their diet, the Seris are a tall race. Their historical good nutrition has made them a handsome people, as well. It is no myth that they can be a fierce-looking bunch, particularly as they appeared several decades ago. The men wore their hair long, often with no thought given to combing it. Food was sometimes scarce, water even scarcer and wearing only their apron-like breechclout, they were every bit as wild, lean and hungry as they appeared.

Women's dress, while modest and colorful, did not detract from the aura of primitiveness. Once a girl achieved puberty she wore a blouse of a solid color, usually red or blue, with borders outlined in contrasting colors to emphasize the contours of the blouse. All women wore long skirts and usually wore scarves. The costume gave an air of the exotic as well as the primitive. Young children, especially boys, went naked. The women's costumes remain largely unchanged today. One of the most striking images I have of the Seris is a rainbow of colors moving across the shimmering desert as a group of women approached, bringing carvings for me to buy.

At times the Seris suffered severe deprivations, lacking food, water and clothing. In the earlier part of this century, when tourists or outsiders appeared, they would be rushed by a desperate group hoping for gifts, throwaways or even scraps of food, a most frightening experience for the tourists. If there were goods to be distributed, the Indians scrambled to get as much as possible in a scene reminiscent of children scurrying at the breaking of a piñata.

On top of their sometimes fierce appearance, their language sounds gutteral to the English speaker, full of sounds unknown in either Spanish or English. The kind of scene such a group would make against a backdrop of convenient tales of cannibalism lent itself to the perpetuation of a myth.

Yet, in all the time I spent with the Seris, I never witnessed any actual violence. It was there, potentially, particularly when alcohol was present. I know it occurred, for there have been homicides, and small-town rumors about one fight or another have been preserved for years. Threats were not uncommon. But violent acts were quite rare.

The Seris have ways of dealing with explosive situations. Strong social pressure against violent acts taking place results in strong remedies. When, many years ago, a fight resulted in the death of a young man, the combatant's family was required to give to the family of the dead man the next baby born. The child grew up as part of the adoptive family. I was

Angelita Torres

fortunate enough to come to know both families and admired the ease with which both accepted her.

For the most part, the Seris' battle for survival leaves little time for fights among themselves. It is not that Seris have a communal society, for theirs is the most individualistic I know. They hold their lands communally only through policy of the Mexican government. Sharing material wealth is almost unknown outside the extended family, while inside the extended family the sharing of items is regulated by a rigidly defined system. In spite of centuries of inbreeding, which results in everyone ultimately being related to everyone else, there is little community spirit, a factor which may work to their detriment in the face of the onslaught of the dominant, consumer-oriented Mexican culture that threatens to engulf and absorb them.

Even now they are heavily hooked into a cash economy and depend upon Mexican vendors for most of their material culture. In order to obtain the necessary cash for their purchases, they must sell their goods— carvings, baskets and fish—and for this they need reliable customers. So trade is irresistably breaking down their traditional isolation. The merchant, as always, breaks down barriers, but affects uniformity. I brought to the Seris many items they would otherwise have had difficulty obtaining. In so doing I heightened their consumer consciousness and made them more dependent upon goods produced elsewhere, hastening loss of their ability to produce artifacts for their own use.

Adaptation to the extreme aridity of their environment was the key to the Seri's existence, and this environment has long been a cause of their isolation and a barrier to their travelling long distances. Until this century, trade with other peoples was minimal. To the north lies a vast desert, teeming with desert life but with almost no water. To the south the land is even more arid. Between the Río Sonora, which drains into the Gulf south of Kino Bay and the usually dry Guaymas River sixty miles further south, springs are found in only two or three places immediately adjacent to the ocean. Inland is a vast desert wilderness. Their only means of transportation, besides their feet, lay in their reed boats called *balsas*. The Seris responded by developing an intimacy with the Gulf coast.

They fashioned balsas from reeds that grow around the springs on Isla Tiburón. They studied the habits of marine animals. They became experts on tides and currents. They analysed the winds, identifying at least seven types, each with its own climatic implications. They undertook expeditions to other islands in the Gulf, exploring them with minute scrutiny, searching for water sources and food. From native materials they developed effective tools and weapons for obtaining food and materials from the sea and the land. They experimented endlessly with the myriad of available plant and animal substances, developing a huge inventory of pharmacological knowledge. Even today their storehouse of natural lore is phenomenal.

The nomadic life continued well into this century, even into the 1980s, but as nomads they were doomed. They preferred a life of ordered wanderings which corresponded largely with the movement of various marine species of fish, turtles and shellfish. Yet their nomadic inclinations were limited by the availability of fresh water. If the fish were running in an area where lack of rain meant drinking water was unavailable, they could move to the spot only on a temporary basis. Mexican culture offered permanent water and supplies. To enjoy these conveniences, the nomadic life had to go. Then as the tourist market made basket weaving and wood sculpting the sources of wealth, the wandering lifestyle was left behind. A large basket may take a year to make and it can't be hauled all over the Gulf during weaving.

In the early 1900s, the Seris learned from Mexicans how to build fishing boats. These replaced the highly manueverable but tiny balsas they had used for centuries. Bulky and unwieldy, the flat-bottomed Mexican design was, nevertheless, safer and bigger and, because it was fitted first with sails, later with motors, it was superior as a fishing boat. An entire family could fit into one of the Mexican-type boats while the balsas were an individual affair.

The flat-bottomed design soon gave way to a more streamlined version as the Seris adapted the Mexican boat to their liking. They painted the exteriors with bright enamels, each man (boat construction was strictly a male activity) choosing his own combination so the harbors sometimes resembled a brightly colored carnival. They carved the boat's ribs with mesquite, which would last forever and used rough pine for the exterior, a happy combination of native and imported materials. They could stand in these boats, manipulate their gear, and harpoon turtles with relative ease. They learned to use nets and monofilament fishing line along with artificial lures.

But these boats, too, were doomed. In the middle 1970s the Mexican government advanced considerable sums of money for the purchase of fiberglass boats to assist the Seris in modernizing their fishing resources.

A fiberglass boat is lighter, faster, more maneuverable and more durable than a wooden boat. It is also ugly, or at least not very attractive. Since the boats are purchased, and not individually constructed by the owner, the art of boat building is becoming a thing of the past. Gone forever are the days when an idler like myself could sit for hours on the beach and watch a craftsman carefully shape a heavy slab of mesquite into the rib of a boat, observing the careful placement of the planks onto it. The harbor of Desemboque now resembles any other small harbor in Mexico. The rainbow of colors that made it distinctly Seri is gone. The new boats also seem to be less permeated by the smell of fish. Who knows whether we should rejoice or grieve?

While occasionally individuals can make a quick bundle of cash when there is a sudden run of sea turtles, scallops or octopus, it is apparent to many men that they can usually make better money carving than fishing. They also cannot compete with modern Mexican and Japanese fishing trawlers. Experts tell me that these modern boats, with their sophisticated technology, have seriously depleted the fish population of the Gulf of California, once the finest fishing area in the world according to many fishermen.

Only seldom do Seri boats come as they once did, laden with scores of flopping fish. One almost never sees the 50- to 60-pound totuava or the 80- to 100-pound groupers that were such a lucrative catch. The bottom of the Gulf, so intimately intertwined with the marine ecological balance, has been irreversibly altered by the scraping of the shrimp boats which provide delicacies for the affluent gourmets of the United States and of Mexico. Now only triggerfish, considered a trash fish by commercial fishermen but a delicacy by the Seris, are on the increase.

As the Seris have adapted to changing conditions around them, their culture has also changed. The Seri's religion tells a lot about their way of life, for they join the Lacandon Maya in being the only Indian group in Mexico that did not experience wholesale conversion to Catholicism. Their historical religion is vague, polytheistic and unsystematic and it does not appear to play an unequivocally important role in their lives; the church and the clergy were never central figures in Seri village life the way they were in Catholic towns.

Themes and practices run through their culture that are important and could be called spiritual, such as songs to control the wind and ceremonies to certain creatures in order to placate their powers. These are not highly organized however, or in the case of the mandatory dancing upon the capture of a leatherback sea-turtle, they are not tied into any monolithic world-view. Seris do not worship, at least as we normally conceive of worship. Some of their dances are carried out as preventive medicine. Their songs to the wind are manipulative. Their reverence for nature, as seen by their respect for dolphins, coyotes and boojum-trees, might be called a religious attitude, but it is not one of formal worship. Their attitudes toward nature have always struck me as being pervaded with a mystical respect. There is a deep, but unstated awareness of a certain sanctity that nature is presumed to merit.

I don't want to give the impression that the Seris are free of religious influences. Years ago a fundamentalist Mexican Protestant group was successful in converting some of the Indians and today almost all who live in Desemboque have had some contact with the Christian religion. Many attend religious services, although some of these probably more out of the entertainment value than out of zeal. Many went to church for a while and then stopped.

Yet the church's influence has been at least linguistically pervasive. Most Seris talk about "heaven," "Jesus Christ," "God" and other such terminology typically associated with Christianity. There does not appear to be any systematic attempt by them to organize religion into their daily lives, however. Numerous clergy have come and gone, some of them fine, honest men. None seems to have left behind much individual influence. The use of alcohol, forbidden by the church, noticeably declined in those times when the church has been active, a clear benefit to the Seri people.

Far more influential have been the two missionaries from the Summer Institute of Linguistics, Ed (now deceased) and Becky Moser. They resided in Desemboque for more than thirty years, committed to their goal of translating the Bible into the Seri language. The Mosers have had a strong influence, not only because of their religious zeal and their monumental achievement of publishing a Seri Bible, but also because through them the Seris experienced continuous contact with North American cultural practices. The Mosers appear to have escaped the stinging attacks on the Summer Institute of Linguistics by nationalistic and progressive political groups that have curtailed the Institute's programs elsewhere. As a result of their work, the Seri language is now written and permanent, an invaluable factor in favor of the preservation of their culture. The Seris read the Bible in their language. They write in their language.

The Seris' culture is being weakened, not by religious movements or outside customs, but by the more powerful pressures of economic and material forces. The mass media, consumerism and trade relentlessly seek to force the Seris into the mainstream of mass, urban oriented society. Increasingly their ideals are those they have heard voiced on their radios or seen on the television screens that hypnotize them when they visit Hermosillo. I was astonished one day when one of the Seri men took me aside and asked me to get him some vitamins.

"But Ramón, do you really want vitamins?"

"Si, Daveed. But the vitamins I want are special vitamins."

"What sort of special vitamins do you need?"

"Mayo Vitamins. They are very good for you".

"Mayo Vitamins?" I thought of the Mayo Indians. What in the world could he be talking about?

"Si, Daveed. Mayo Vitamins. They come from the United States."

I assured him I would try to find some. But then, as I wrote down his request so as not to forget it, I decided that I would simply get a brand of multiple vitamins that would surely do the job.

That night I happened to be listening to a Mexican radio program. Soon a commercial came on, advertising, of course, Mayo Vitamins, produced in Los Angeles and pandered on a Mexican radio station in Tijuana. The commercial assured that those who consumed Mayo Vitamins would be healthier, better looking and happier and these benefits would extend even more surely to their children. The commercial was obviously working. The next day I told Ramón that I could get him vitamins but no Mayos. He left me in disgust.

The Seris long, just as the rest of us do, to be glamorous, brilliant and comfortable, as are the movie stars they see glorified in the media; and they assume, as we do, that buying into the mass market of fine clothes, automobiles, cosmetics and popular foods will help achieve this goal.

Yet, in spite of all these powerful influences, the Seris retain a strong cultural identity. For the time being, they are still Seris; they speak Seri and regard their land as their life and the edge of the sea as the edge of their destiny. Their home continues to be identified as the place where the desert meets the sea. Alien forces, such as those represented by Mexicans (to whom they refer as "Yoris," a somewhat derogatory term) and North Americans (who are viewed as rather daft), are still seen as things to be tolerated, used for Seri purposes and otherwise ignored except when their resources are needed. The real challenge will come when television arrives in Desemboque. That time may not be far away.

And so, in this computer age, even with the arrival of cassette recorders and processed and pre-packed foods into the Seri homes and of pickup trucks parked outside, the spirit of the ancient Seris lives on. If you are fortunate enough to be on the beach of Desemboque at sunset, you may still hear the soft murmur of Seri voices, the sharp echo of the chipping of ironwood and the gentle sound of Seri songs as the sun goes down over the edge of the world.

Seriland

It was by accident that I first found my way into Seri country. During the long summer of 1968 I had been involved in Tucson, Arizona with the frantic political activity revolving around the Vietnam War that culminated in the Democratic National Convention in Chicago. At the time, I was 27 and an instructor at the University of Arizona. The end of the summer session coincided with an emotional letdown as the political process yielded results I viewed as inevitably disastrous. I desperately wanted to get away from my home in Tucson and spend some time in the wilderness, preferably in Mexico.

I had believed for some time that it would be a challenge to take a trip into the Sierra Madre in Mexico to an area I had heard tales about. I had become friends with Mikki Niemi, a wildlife biologist and one of my students, particularly after he had helped overhaul the engine on my Land Rover. Mikki was a powerfully-built, tough outdoorsman and he seemed an appropriate companion for an expedition into the wilds of Mexico, an escape into primitive nature.

Mikki jumped at the idea. My Land Rover, awaiting the arrival of parts from England, couldn't make it, but Mikki believed his old Jeep station wagon was up to the rigors we would encounter in the bush. We planned to leave in a couple of days.

I spent a good part of the next day poring over maps of the Sierra Madre. Supposedly there was no route over the range between the paved drive from Durango to Mazatlan and the casual dirt road just south of the U.S.

border, linking Sonora with Chihuahua. In other words, for 700 miles there was no identifiable crossing. But I did locate what looked like a Jeep trail beginning near Ciudad Obregon, Sonora and ending up in Chihuahua City, a distance of more than 300 miles. I also learned that in the area were two distinct Indian groups, Pima Bajos, who make fine baskets, called *guari*, and Tarahumaras, who are known as the mountain and canyon Indians of Mexico. Both of us were interested in Indians and a visit to these tribes of the remote Sierra sounded like the adventure we were seeking. We decided to attempt a crossing over that undescribed route.

Mikki had travelled extensively in Mexico and spoke fairly decent Spanish. I had learned the language in my travels in Mexico and in the streets of Tucson and had polished up with a few college courses. Since we had both heard stories of *gabachos* (outsiders) being shot at in the Sierra Madre by enterprising drug dealers, we considered it prudent to have some fluency in the local dialect.

Early the next morning we threw our trappings into the Jeep and were ready to depart. I kissed my wife Patsy and our son Chris goodbye and we chugged off.

We didn't get far. At the gas station Mikki noticed a drip underneath the gas tank. A rock had made a hole, creating a leak—small enough now, but guaranteed to increase in size in direct proportion to the penetration of the uninhabited wilderness of the Sierra Madre. We returned to Mikki's house, removed all our gear from the Jeep and went to work. Repairing the hole devoured most of the day and we didn't leave until late afternoon. It wasn't an auspicious start.

Twelve hours later we camped for the night in a mesquite forest in the foothills of the Sierra Madre. The mosquitos were abominable, not to mention the myriad of other biting and buzzing creatures activated by the monsoon rains. As biting insects find my blood especially tasty, I was forced to string up a jungle hammock with netted sides. It took me the better part of an hour to set up the contraption. Mikki, much hardier than I, slapped on some insect repellent, rolled up in a light blanket and fell dead asleep almost before I had the hammock unpacked from the Jeep.

We rose early in the morning and headed east on a primitive road into what was new country for both of us, crossing low mountain ranges and valleys populated by only a few peasants and ranchers. As we penetrated more deeply into the foothills of the Sierra, we found the summer rains had swollen dry washes into creeks and creeks into rivers. Once we got stuck for a half hour in water that reached the floorboards of the Jeep. Twice we stalled while crossing another watercourse and had to climb out into knee-deep water in order to dry off the distributor contacts. We solved this problem later when a passing Mexican truck driver advised us that pouring oil over the distributor would prevent water from getting inside. That worked, all right, but made a mess of the engine. Were the gods sending us a message?

As we lumbered upward through the foothills, the road became progressively worse. We managed little more than a few miles per hour. Suddenly we reached a stretch where the road looked as though it had been recently plowed. Foot-deep ruts were filled with standing water and mud, and an impenetrable forest of thorny trees and vines stood on each side. Mikki slammed the Jeep into 4-wheel drive and we slogged through, sliding and slipping, as the wheels churned the muck into an even greater mess.

At the other side of the bog Mikki suggested we check the undercarriage of the Jeep. I got down, looked underneath and was disheartened to see oil oozing from the pinion seal on the drive shaft. That was ominous. Mikki carefully loosened the drain plug on the differential. Water spurted out.

We were in trouble. The differential had filled with water while we were stuck in the last creek. Sooner or later the entire rear end would freeze up. We had no choice. We had to turn back. The gods had spoken.

Miraculously, we made it back through the bog and across all the rivers and by late afternoon arrived in the city of Navojoa where a mechanic drained the differential and replaced the water with oil. No apparent damage to the spider gears or the ring and crown, he said. But we had lost a couple of days and had only three left. What to do?

"Say, Dave," Mikki remarked over a beer in a *cantina* in Navojoa, "have you ever been to visit the Seris?" I owned I hadn't, although I had heard of them, as has anyone who has frequented the back roads of Sonora. "Well, they're a real trip. They make great ironwood carvings and think that gringos are crazy. Let's go visit them."

That was enough for me. Although it meant a complete change of plans and direction and would require a sweltering ride, I was game. We headed north by night, back through Ciudad Obregón, up through the Yaqui country to Guaymas and then to Bahia Kino where we found a place to camp.

I make the trip sound easy, but a problem had developed with the Jeep's steering so that it tended to meander all over the highway. Mikki managed to keep the Jeep under control, but not without immense effort and considerable profanity.

I was glad he was driving, both because I don't especially like to drive and because it took a good deal of strength to control the Jeep. Mikki is very strong, but even so we swerved a couple of times in the direction of oncoming trucks, not a good policy in Mexico. Mexican truck drivers have a strong macho instinct and tend to think you are playing "chicken" when they see you head for them, and they are usually willing to call your bluff.

In fact, the craziness of the traffic is such that one should always have all possible resources available to avoid devastating and frequently fatal calamaties. Casual meandering across the center line is normal for many large vehicles, as numerous North Americans have discovered all too late. It was one o'clock in the morning when we reached Kino Bay. Mikki was tired of fighting the Jeep and ready to sack out. Worried about the steering, we checked the mechanism underneath the Jeep. We found a couple of loose bolts which we tightened, but it was clear the ball joints were badly worn, not an easy item to repair under the best of circumstances. Oh, well, Mikki philosophized, tomorrow most of the trip would be on dirt roads where the meander wouldn't amount to much.

Morning found us headed north to Punta Chueca, the southernmost Seri village. This desert area is magnificent, with large organ pipe cactus and a strange giant called the cardón *(Pachycereus pringlei)*, larger and hardier than the huge saguaro cactus so well known in the southwestern U. S. and found only in Sonora and Baja California. Also in abundance was a strange bush called the elephant tree *(Bursera microphylla)* whose massive, fleshy trunk is seldom more than ten feet high. Along the washes were ironwood trees, which in spite of low rainfall, manage to attain ages of several hundred years. The country was vast, magnificent and almost unpopulated.

Punta Chueca was a strange sight. It consisted of fifty or so huts, if they might be called that, made of an asphalt-impregnated corrugated cardboard. Many Indians emerged from these huts as we drove into town. Most of them headed toward the Jeep, waving wooden figurines in our faces and offering a few fibre baskets and necklaces made of shell and bone.

The Indians were certainly picturesque. Most of the men had long hair and the women wore colorful blouses with full, brightly-dyed skirts. They matched the descriptions I had read of Seris as wildlooking, primitive people. They also bore a peculiar smell, which I was later able to identify as a mixture of ironwood smoke and cooking fish. I have come to love that particular smell.

Elfraín Estrella   *Herminia Astorga*   *María Luisa Astorga*

The crowd of Indians overwhelmed me and they were none too gentle in insisting that I buy their wares. It was clear they intended to make a sale. A couple of women jabbed me in the ribs continuously, staring with baleful looks that bordered on threatening. I smiled uneasily and looked hopefully toward Mikki, who shrugged his powerful shoulders and grinned; he had spent a lot of time here while conducting research in nearby estuaries and was enjoying my discomfort.

I paid for a couple of necklaces, spurning persistent clamoring that I buy carvings so the vendor might buy food that night. Mikki had suggested that carvings would be better and cheaper in Desemboque, which lay well to the north. After politely examining a couple of baskets and a few carvings, we jumped in the Jeep. Several women followed us and pushed their wares in the window of the Jeep, denouncing us as heartless beasts I am sure, in what was to me incomprehensible Seri.

Soon we were on the road again, paralleling the Infernillo Channel. Much more difficult than the previous one, the road wound its way through sand and low hills, then out onto flats and back into sand. Mikki managed to steer the Jeep, but we still crashed back and forth along broad ruts so deep the sand occasionally scraped the vehicle's bottom.

Although somewhat familiar with the area, Mikki wasn't sure exactly how far we had to go. It was fearfully hot and the sand treacherous. Several times the wheels spun and we bogged down as we labored through a dry wash. After an hour or so we were long past a mountain that Mikki had pointed out as the landmark for navigating one's way to Desemboque. The village was just the other side of that mountain, he had promised. But now the landmark was fading into the background as the road became worse, hardly more than a sandy dry wash carved into oxbows. I said nothing, but had long since begun to doubt that we were on the right road.

Suddenly we came upon a village, hardly more than a few shacks and trees, but at any rate a sign of civilization. We pulled up near a couple of huts, and, covered with dust and sweat, climbed out of the Jeep, thankful to be in a village, even one as miserable as Desemboque appeared to be.

We weren't out of the Jeep more than a few seconds when Indians converged upon us, seeming to materialize from nowhere. Soon thirty or forty gathered around, showing us carvings, many of which were excellent. Unlike the Seris from Punta Chueca, these people were smiling and laughing; perhaps they knew no outsiders in their right mind would make such a long journey and leave without buying a few carvings.

Before long Mikki and I were engaged in conversation. The women, who were doing most of the selling, seemed to understand my Spanish but spoke only in the crisp, musical Seri language. They were glad we had come, for they truly needed to sell their wares to buy food. I bought a few exquisite figurines and shell necklaces, along with a small basket.

Then I looked around and visually embraced Desemboque for the first time. Situated on a broad bay, with stark, dramatic mountains in the background, it has a simple, primitive feel to it. Something about it was hauntingly attractive, something I couldn't express.

Sixty or so huts were scattered along the beach, with a handful of more or less permanent buildings set back a little farther. A few salt cedars gave a bit of shade here and there, and fifteen or twenty boats graced the harbor. That was it. I felt the Indians themselves—primitive enough in appearance and with an exotic language to boot—gave the village a touch of romanticism, something out of Gauguin, especially if one could ignore the fact that their clothes were rather dirty, the children were clothed mostly in rags and the ground was littered with what appeared to be many years' accumulation of miscellaneous trash.

I joined Mikki, who moved among the Indians with the ease of an experienced anthropologist. We walked around the town for a couple of hours, chatting and, before long, joking with the Seris. The huts, haphazard as they seemed and cluttered with what appeared to be discarded artifacts, were highly organized around the Indians' outdoor life. What had appeared at first to be chaos was order. At first I thought the objects scattered on the ground had been randomly abandoned. In reality, everything was in its place. It was a new experience for me. Here was a people who lived without any pretext of conventional neatness, but who obviously heartily enjoyed life and were comfortable in what I had assumed would be an inhospitable environment. The village began to take on a meaning for me.

As the sun began to move toward the western horizon, we headed back toward Tucson. As we left, I told a couple of the Indians, "I'll be back soon."

They smiled.

Trading with José

When I first visited Desemboque on that hot summer day, it was, as it is now (depending on the time of year), a village of between 200 and 400 people. At that time it was fifty miles to the nearest permanent human settlement, and isolated from other villages by the vast sweeps of the Gulf coast portion of the Sonoran Desert. I felt a great relief encountering the village after crossing the parched desert.

Desemboque del Río San Ignacio is situated on a broad bay in the Gulf of California. The nearby San Ignacio River, or more accurately, dry wash, is the terminal point of a huge drainage system originating in an inland water system. While the river runs only for a couple of hours every few years, water is permanently available in wells near the wash's mouth. To the southwest is a fine view of Tepopa Point, while just beyond one can catch a glimpse of Isla Tiburón, the Seri's ancestral homeland and refuge from the attacks of Spaniards and Mexicans. At the time of my first visit most of the huts were situated within a few hundred feet or so of the high water mark and built so that each door opened onto the wide expanse of the sea.

It was on that first trip that I met José Astorga, entrepreneur, mystic, apostate and tyrant, probably still the Seri best known to the outside world.

As founder of ironwood carving and an innovator of sculptural styling, José is held in awe by numerous Seris and in scorn by others. A spinner of tall tales, many of his yarns are accepted as fact. Some Seris report that he has been to the moon.

Several years ago José chose to move his home several miles inland, completely out of view of the ocean, an action unheard of among the Seris. His stated reason? He wanted to be a rancher, although no Seri has ever undertaken any agricultural projects. The real reason had something to do with his being asked to watch over the village well, because the well pump kept breaking down. It may also have had something to do with his eccentricity and his alleged supernatural powers. After a short period of time, José returned to the village. The pump kept going out anyway.

José claims that as a young man he was inducted into the Mexican armed forces. He was gone from Seri country for several years, during which time, as he tells it, he lost much of his ability to speak Seri. Other Seris, including his wife, say he never left Seri country. Nevertheless, today he sometimes seems more comfortable speaking Spanish than his native Seri. Most people who know him well agree he is not a typical Seri.

José reports that sometime in his later life (he was in his early fifties when I first met him) he underwent a mystical experience. As he and his sons much later related, he was attracted to a cave on Cerro Pelón, a mountain about five miles inland from Desemboque. Inside the cave he fasted and did not sleep for several days. During that time a spirit with a bat-like appearance visited him. The spirit instructed him to begin to carve ironwood in order to save his people, suggesting the actual forms he should carve.

Although histories differ (others claim the idea of carving ironwood was suggested by a North American visitor), it is clear José began to experiment with carving ironwood in the early 1960s. His first experiments were dismal failures, but he learned rapidly and soon began to produce figures resembling Eskimo soapstone sculptures, although Eskimo art was unknown to him. His family helped him and together they began to produce many high quality sculptures.

Ironwood *(Olneya tesota)* is the hardest and one of the two densest woods found on our continent, the other being leadwood, found in Florida. It grows abundantly in the Sonoran Desert below 2400 feet elevation and particularly flourishes in the deserts of the state of Sonora, Mexico. It can withstand both sparse rainfalls (frequently less than three inches annually in the Desemboque area and even less farther north) and temperatures that reach 120 degrees.

Live wood is not suitable for carving. Only pieces that have been dead, the longer dead the better, will do. Frequently a tree has a dead portion with a massive trunk that shows not the slightest sign of decay although death may have occurred several centuries ago, while the living part of the tree flourishes. The aged, dead wood is so hard and dense it appears to be fossilized. This wood is the best for carving.

Carving of ironwood is no simple task. It is probably more accurate to refer to the figurines as sculptures rather than carvings. The dense grain resists any carving by knife and the excess wood must be chipped away.

The resulting figure, when properly done, has a grace and beauty unique among Indian art forms. Ironwood seems specially suited for sculpture. Its deep, brown color, when polished, gleams like opal. The more skilled artists now produce birds in flight, dolphins jumping from the water, sea lions cavorting on rocks and Seri dancers. Their art is all the more remarkable in that, in Desemboque at least, the artists use only primitive hand tools— the machete remains the basic sculpting tool.

The Seris are now internationally renowned for their sculptures, as they should be, and much has been written about Seri ironwood carvings. Their success has inspired imitation elsewhere, but no imitators have managed to match the Seris' ability to capture in ironwood the spirit of desert and sea creatures.

Few realize that the development of the art form is due primarily to the peculiar genius of José Astorga whom I was lucky enough to have met on that hot, sultry August day in 1968. That was the first of nearly one hundred trips I have made in the intervening years.

Part of the mystique associated with José is his appearance. A short man, his striking face, with its large nose and very prominent cheekbones, is

José Astorga

reminiscent of the facial features of the Maya Indians. His demeanor is strongly Indian and at first his mode of communication is through slow, deliberate responses; only later does his great sense of humor emerge. For years he wore the hat of a military policeman, a trademark that enhanced his fame.

José is as shrewd a businessman as any Seri. While his diverse investments are modest by North American standards, he is constantly producing schemes to make money. He once conned me into buying into his herd of goats.

"Aye, Javid (his strange pronounciation of my name), you should buy a chiva (goat)."

"Why should I do that?"

"Because if you do, pretty soon there will be three."

"And what will I do with three chivas?"

"Keep them. Pretty soon they will be ten or twenty."

"Then what will I do with them?"

"Sell them to Mexicans. They're not very smart and will pay a lot."

When I resisted his hard sell routine, he tried a more subtle method.

"Aye, Javid. Loan me two hundred pesos ($16)."

"No way, you old coyote. You still haven't paid me back the two hundred I loaned you last trip."

"But I need money to buy some medicine for Rosa (his wife)."

"You tell me what the medicine is and I'll buy it."

"Aye, Javid, you talk just like the other gringos. We are poor, we Seris. Give me a hundred pesos and I promise you I'll make you a nice carving of a sea lion."

"No, you give me the carving first, then I'll give you a hundred pesos."

"Look, you bastard, we're hungry and don't have any money. You're a rich gringo. Give me fifty pesos and I'll give you a chivo (buck)."

"All right, José, I'll give you a hundred pesos and you give me a chiva (doe)."

"No, you give me three hundred pesos and I'll let you have two of my best chivas and soon you'll be a rich man.

"All right, I'll give you two hundred pesos and three of those chivas are mine."

"Aye, Javid, you take advantage of me. You can have three of the best."

And so it happened. I bought three head, accepting naively his line that they would soon be six and then twelve and I would one day be a rich man.

Foolishly, however, I neglected to go over to his herd and mark my choices. A month or so later I made another trip to Desemboque. After speaking with him for an hour or so the conversation turned to the goats.

"How are my chivas, José?"

"Aye, Javid, I have bad news for you."

Bad news. I just couldn't guess. I prepared to strangle him.

"Javid, es que los coyotes las mataron." (The coyotes had killed them.)

Strange, I thought, looking out at the little corral behind his hut. The herd looked just as big to me.

And how many had the coyotes killed? Well, he told me, deep sadness furrowing his already wrinkled brow, three had been eaten by coyotes.

"And those three just happened to be the three I bought from you?"

"Si, Javid. Sometimes all of us have bad luck."

But all was not lost, he assured me. He just happened to have three others that he would sell me at a most reasonable price . . .

I found out about many of Jose's enterprises because he, as well as many other Series, would ask me (from time to time) to make mathematical calculations. In those days, electronic calculators had not been invented and my ability to do mental conversions from one currency to another was highly sought after by the Seris.

Sometimes José's plans for increasing his revenues were ingenious. When a Mexican drove a road grader near town, José paid him a few hundred pesos to blade off an airstrip just north of the village. Thus was born José's airport. He tricked somebody out of an old wind sock and he was in business. When another North American friend, Ike Russell, suggested the need for maintenance, José requested that Ike make him a sign. Ike, a strong supporter and long-time friend of the Seris, flew down a week or so later. The Seris would always rush out to the airstrip when a plane landed and this visit was no exception.

Disembarking from the plane, Ike handed José a nicely painted sign which read: "This airstrip has been maintained by José Astorga. Please help by contributing ten pesos." Ike was proud and José even prouder of the sign as he had one of his children read it for him. Then as he and Ike walked toward the village José stopped him.

"By the way," he said, holding out his hand, "the sign says, ten pesos." Ike paid.

Then there was the saga of my house in Desemboque. After eight or ten trips I grew tired of camping on the beach and thought it would be a good idea if I had access to a more permanent habitation. I found a place where I could build right on the beach and mentioned it to José.

"Aye, Javid, you should build a casita right next to my house."

"Why should I do that when I like the beach better?"

"Because, silly gringo, here it will be safer. No one will be able to steal from your house because we will always be watching it and it won't be blown down by storms."

I had to admit his points made sense, so I marked off an area right next to his house and paid him a couple of hundred pesos for the land. Then his son Santiago and I figured out the configuration and prepared the plans.

Over the next couple of months I plowed a few thousand pesos into the building. I bought cement, laminated aluminum roofing and window jams in Hermosillo, 120 miles away, and laboriously hauled them to the village. I then deposited more money with Santiago to pay the workers and told him I would like construction to begin.

I returned a couple of weeks later and sure enough, the foundations had been poured and the walls were beginning to rise. I was proud that I would own one of the few permanent dwellings in the village and would have a nice place to stay on my trips. And everyone would know where David's house was. I would gain permanence and respect.

On the next trip the walls were a little higher, but not much. I inquired from Santiago as to what the problem was.

"Well, Daveed, the workers want more money and we need more blocks." (Who were the workers? José's sons.) I forked over a few hundred more pesos, pleading with him to see to it that work progressed more rapidly.

My next trip was about a month later. Very little work had been done. I began to get a little testy with José.

"Look, you coyote, you have my money, where is my house?"

"Don't get alarmed, Javid, your house will get built. But things are very expensive nowadays. Give me a couple hundred more pesos and the house will be yours."

I reluctantly handed over more money, warning him that this was the last time. I walked away seething, knowing there was nothing I could do. Completion of the house was in his hands. If I threatened, he would just do nothing and there was no way I could force the issue.

Unfortunately for me, summer followed and I was unable to return to Desemboque for a couple of months. When I was able to make the trip, I was eager to see my house. I had visions of a nice cottage with a snug roof, a neat concrete floor, a solid door and a divider between the rooms. I rushed into town and headed for the spot where my house should be, having to use the headlights since it was dark.

The walls were almost unchanged, not more than three feet high. A doorway had been fashioned, but was blocked by a primitive gate. I stopped the Rover near the front and walked toward the partially-constructed building. From inside I heard the bleat of a goat. I walked to a wall and peered inside. There was a herd of goats, apparently being kept safe from coyotes inside the unfinished walls of my house. Goats! And not *my* goats, either. I walked around to José's yard. He was sitting on his veranda, carving to the light of a Coleman lantern. He hardly looked up when I walked in, although I hadn't seen him for months. He hacked away at a chunk of ironwood.

"Listen, cabrón, what have you done to my house?"

"Aye, Javid, you've had bad luck again. The government won't let foreigners build houses here in Desemboque. To finish it we would have to ask permission of the government and you would really get into trouble when they see you began it without permission. Better just leave it alone before they make more trouble for you."

I was beginning to get angry, but knew I had no appeal. "All right, you thief, but where is my roofing? I paid 700 pesos for it."

"Oh, that stuff. I knew you wouldn't be using it so I sold it to a Yori (a Mexican)."

"Thanks a lot," I muttered sarcastically. "You're welcome," he added, not understanding my sarcasm. "So I have no house. Please let me have the money you got for the roofing."

"Of course. I got you a really good deal. I made them pay 500 pesos for it."

"500 pesos? I paid 700 pesos for it!"

"Yes, but you know how things are here."

"Okay, at least give me my 500 pesos."

"Aye, Javid. I don't have it, but I have some fine carvings here and I'll give you a real good price instead . . ."

To this day I have no house in Desemboque.

It is hard, though, to be enterprising without broadening one's horizons and searching for new ways to make a few pesos. In José's case it has contributed to the breakdown of the culture in a way that even transistor radios and high-powered advertising cannot.

Unlike many cultures in the world, the birth of a girl is a cause for greater joy for a Seri father than the birth of a male child. Nowadays, because of her future earning capacity, a girl can mean just as much potential economic prosperity to a family as the birth of a boy; the sale of baskets and necklaces, made exclusively by women, can match or exceed sales of ironwood figurines. And while few young men carve, preferring to hang around indolently, most young girls of the same age also carve or polish carvings, thus supplementing the family income. A skilled young female carver, and there are several of them, can produce an astonishing number of fine carvings.

Even more important, however, a daughter means a bride price when she is of marriageable age. Among the Seris, bride prices have always been steep. Until recently the going rate for a bride would be tools, baskets, some figurines, a little money, new clothes and some important artifacts, locally produced.

José was instrumental in upping the ante on bride prices, so today, to marry one of his daughters, the suitor's family must produce a new pickup truck, a radio or other appliances and several hundred thousand pesos. The custom degenerated into a virtual buying and selling of commodities to the extent that some brides have been priced right out of the market.

In the earliest years of my adventures with the Seris, I became close friends with several members of José's family. One of his six daughters was twenty-nine and unmarried when I met her for the first time, a rather advanced age for a Seri woman to find herself still a señorita. It was not until I knew the family well that she told me that she had been promised for years as a bride to a hard-working Seri man. She had no particular desire to marry him, but all had been arranged.

Then I learned that the "arrangement" consisted of the fact that the suitor's family had agreed to pay José what seemed to me an exhorbitant price for the "privilege" of marrying his daughter. Payment in money, goods and services had continued for several years. The potential injustice of it all was that José could, at any time, change his mind, forbid the marriage and still keep the bride price already advanced. In other words, payment of the bride price was no guarantee of a bride.

The couple did marry and today have a large family. (It was falsely rumored that their first child, one of the darkest Seri babies I have ever seen, was the result of a liaison between her and me. After seventeen years, the rumor, preposterous as it is, shows not the slightest sign of abating.)

But some of her younger sisters have not been so fortunate. I am told that José asked such outrageous bride prices for these other daughters that no families were interested. As a result, two of the three, on their own, married Mexican men who are unimpressed with either bride prices or Seri customs. The third remained unmarried into her late twenties although she is bright, lovely and clearly marriageable.

José may be getting a bit desperate as a later conversation will show. Years after my divorce I spent a week or so in the village and became rather smitten with Irmadelia, his youngest daughter. One day she and I spent several hours talking together, outside her house. The next day José was carving in his old house when I came by.

"Javid, you aren't married, are you?"

"No, José, I'm not."

"Why don't you marry her," he said, pointing to Irmadelia.

"I don't much want to get married again."

"Look, get me a new pickup and two hundred thousand pesos and you will have a fine wife."

"But I don't have two hundred thousand pesos."

"Forget the money. Give me a new pickup and she is yours."

José's "love of the centavo," as they say in Mexico, has had the same effect on his sons. He was apparently unwilling to advance the bride price necessary for them to marry Seri wives. As a consequence, two of them have chosen Mexican wives. While both wives are superior women, one of them being one of four or five non-Seris fluent in the Seri language, the intermarriage tends to increase the Mexicanization of the Seris. Their children are being raised not as Seris, but as Mexicans.

And yet José has made enormous contributions to his people. His visions not only produced ironwood carving, but led him to be receptive to the revival of arts and customs long forgotten. Deer dancing, almost extinct among the Seris, has been revived by him and his sons. Although they had to make a trip to the Yaqui country, a couple of hundred miles to the south to purchase the paraphernalia necessary for the deer dance, they have studied the dance and it appears once again to be a feature of Seri culture. Two of his sons studied the steps of the dance painstakingly and have practiced faithfully. I was present one evening when they danced. The performance was a hit with the Seris and the few outsiders who were present.

José is also constantly carving or making some new artifact—santos (figurines with a mystical significance), mystic whistles and images of spirits. And he is always prepared to explain the meaning of his creations, explanations which frequently carry an uncanny reality with them, but which are sometimes pure hype, sometimes obscene, always imaginative.

Although some of his schemes were harebrained, he has been an unrepentant visionary, many of whose ideas have spread and taken hold. He and I used to spend hours chewing the fat, dreaming of the wonderful farm we could have on Isla Tiburón. I figured we could raise *pitahaya* fruits;

he suggested wheat. I proposed a few orange trees; he added apples, peaches and tamarinds. I hoped for chile peppers, he added cows. I expressed a hope for a limit to a few families. He wanted it for all Seris and the few Mexicans who met with his approval and, of course, every gringo willing to pay the price.

These discussions were the more remarkable for the fact that the only agriculture I have ever seen the Seris seriously involved in is the cultivation of a few marijuana plants, most of which are stolen before they reach maturity. José at one time had a garden when he lived inland guarding the well, but it was only a temporary affair.

Nor can I ever forget the concern he demonstrated for my family on occasions when I took someone on an emergency trip to Hermosillo or to the clinic at Calle Doce (12th Street). Once when I was asked to take a Seri to the doctor he exhorted me to have my family come over to his house and stay in the shade where they would be safer and more comfortable. While I was gone he was most concerned about the welfare of my son Chris and later advised me on how to make sure he didn't get hurt, advice that I wish I had followed, as I shall relate later. He repeatedly offered his house and the area around his place to me, assuring me I would be safer there and my things wouldn't get stolen.

As an old man José has earned a lot of respect. Rosa Flores, his gentle and motherly wife, beset with arthritis is always by his side, constantly feeding their pet javelina and polishing José's numerous carvings. He has become more crotchety and unpredictable, remains as interested as ever in making money, yet he is still very much a Seri. He has shown a lot more interest in old Seri customs. In 1985 he sang Seri songs all night at a puberty celebration for one of his granddaughters. I was astonished, after leaving him singing at midnight, to awaken in the morning to the sound of his voice carrying over the desert to the edge of the sea.

His personality is again revealed by an incident that occurred in 1984. I had taken a dear friend of mine down to meet the Seris. My friend John was a smoker and as José and I chatted next to John's pickup, John pulled out his pack of cigarettes.

"Give me a cigarette," José requested.

John tossed him the pack.

José examined the pack carefully, pulled out a cigarette, sniffed it, then replaced it in the pack. It was a Menthol Light. He threw them back to John.

"I won't smoke those. They make you queer . . ."

The Sting

"Daveed, dispiértate. El Capitán va muriendo." (David, wake up, they said. Capitán is dying.)

"Que pasó?" (What happened?) I asked, instantly awake and unzipping the netting of the tent. It was normal for some Seri or the other to come looking for me. They would come singly or in groups, asking questions, wanting to sell me something or wanting me to get them something. Sometimes they came just to watch, but this time there was alarm in their voices.

"Le picó alacrán. Va muriendo." A scorpion. The most feared enemy of Seri children. Capitán was only six, old enough to survive most scorpion stings, but still in danger.

"Ponlo in mi carro. Lo llevamos al doctor." (Load him in my Land Rover and we'll take him to a doctor.) Sure, I thought, the doctor in Calle Doce, ninety miles away over mostly winding dirt road. He'll be dead before then.

It had been a hot June night in 1970 in Desemboque. I was spending a few weeks of the summer buying carvings and baskets and learning all I could about the Seris and their land. Patsy my wife, Chris my five year-old son, and I slept in the tiny tent. Next to us under a ramada, slept Suzannah, our recently adopted daughter of six months. She slept in a portable crib, surrounded by mosquito netting. The legs of her crib were submerged in #10 cans filled with water to prevent scorpions from climbing up and stinging her.

The Seris had warned us that if you don't have a net cover over a sleeping child, scorpions will drop out of the ceilings of the shacks and ramadas and sting the child. Better yet, they advise, keep the child sleeping with you at all times. No decent parent will let a baby sleep anywhere but in its mother's arms until it is a couple of years old, anyway. They couldn't figure out all this adoption stuff, either.

But Suzannah was safe and Capitán, son and firstborn of Roberto Campuzano and Aurora Astorga, had been stung. He was Campuzano's pride. Already a skilled fisherman at six years of age, Capitán usually accompanied his traditionalist father on fishing trips.

Prudently, I had slept with my trousers on. (When you may have to be up and about at a moment's notice it does not pay to take your clothes off for sleep.) I shook out my shoes, recalling the many stories I had heard of scorpions, crass opportunists that they are, crawling into shoes and stinging the feet of the unsuspecting owner. I slipped on a shirt, jumped into the Land Rover and raced over to José's house, where Capitán had been staying. I could hear his screams over the noise of the engine.

The entire Astorga household was anxiously waiting. Capitán was already beginning to convulse, the first sign of danger after a scorpion sting. Campuzano, who was holding him, showed me the small but nasty sting mark on the child's stomach. María Luisa, Capitán's maternal aunt, had gone to find some antivenin which was usually available, but the Mexican nurse who would administer the serum was nowhere to be found. We dared not wait. Roberto jumped into the Land Rover with Adolfo Burgos, an uncle, and Amalia Astorga, another aunt, following and bearing the screaming child.

I revved up the engine and threw the Rover into reverse. A shout, "Espérate!" (Hold it.) Luisa had arrived with the antivenin and a syringe of doubtful sterility and ancestry. She hastily injected the liquid into Capitán's dark little bottom. He screamed even more. A crowd had gathered and now watched grimly as we flew out of town, all four wheels spinning in the fine sand of the desert lowlands. Seris report that many children have died from scorpion stings, suffocating as the toxin constricts respiration until no air can pass into the lungs. Those who watched as we departed knew the gravity of the situation. The first hour or so is critical and they would not know until late in the day if Capitán was to survive.

That scorpions are actually so aggressive has not been documented by scientists. They are generally retiring creatures, preferring to be left alone in the dark as they hunt for insects. There is no doubt though, that they will sting willingly and repeatedly if provoked.

The tiny bark scorpion is a particularly insidious pest. Seldom more than an inch or so in length, it is far deadlier than its larger and more evil-looking relatives. It is said to be especially aggressive, and because of its diminutive size can hide in inconspicuous places. The Seris believe that scorpions deliberately seek out young children and babies and sting them. My experience tells me they may be right.

The Sonoran Desert is full of scorpions. They thrive in thatch or in rough roofing timbers, which make the ceiling of the typical Sonoran Desert dwelling ideal for them. A restaurant owner in Kino Bay relates that one evening a scorpion dropped from the thatched roof of his cocktail lounge into the drink of a young woman. She declined to finish the drink. They also abound in vegetation around buildings and readily move from the vegetation to the dwelling in their unending search for insect prey. There are lots and lots of scorpions in Sonora.

The Astorga family knew well the danger from scorpions. Their faces were tense as we rode away. Aurora, Capitán's mother and a famous artist, stayed behind. She had other children to take care of, including one she was nursing. It's a father's job to get medical attention for the children. Meanwhile, José, Capitán's maternal grandfather, began to chip away at a sculpture upon our departure. He believes, along with many others, that he has spiritual power through his work. Perhaps he was trying to imbue his sculpture with a power that would save Capitán's life.

I shouted to Patsy, who was just emerging from the tent as we drove by on our way out of town, to get in the shade. The daytime temperature would reach over 100 degrees and shade was hard to come by in Desemboque.

Without shade, Suzannah would become very sick. Furthermore, Patsy didn't speak much Spanish and understood even less. I was worried about her and our children and how they would fare in my absence, but I had no choice as I was the ambulance driver. It was about 5:45am. We had to leave immediately. We would be fortunate to get to Calle Doce by 8:30.

The ride was interminable. The road winds for miles through deep sand, across ancient dry lakes and over rolling desert *bajada*, with forests of cardón cactus and elephant trees and the sparkling Gulf in the background. Now the whole magnificent panorama seemed to reflect an air of immense and lofty indifference. The government-operated clinic at Calle Doce seemed an eternity away. Even if we found it open, I doubted if we would make it in time to save Capitán's life.

By now Capitán was screaming constantly, "Ita, ita." (Mommy, mommy.) Campuzano, his face as stolid as ever, tried to concentrate on the landscape. Gentle and brooding Amalia, with only a single child of her own, a daughter about Capitán's age, and no prospect for any more, sought to comfort him as the convulsions worsened. Adolfo tried unsuccessfully to keep up a conversation, then gave up. I drove so fast over the narrow, winding dirt road that the others had to hold on to keep from being thrown to the floor of the Rover.

A little more than an hour later, we churned past Punta Chueca, not stopping to talk to anyone. Only an emergency could justify such behavior. Occasionally a doctor would visit Punta Chueca, but nobody wanted to stop and find out if one was there. Stopping would have risked the loss of precious time and Calle Doce was still a good fifty miles away. Capitán still looked deathly ill although it seemed to me that his breathing was less labored.

The road from Punta Chueca to Kino Bay is much better and it is possible to drive about forty-five miles an hour safely. I did sixty, about as fast as the Rover would go. At times the washboard condition of the road jarred us till we felt our teeth would fall out. I glanced over at Campuzano, who had hardly uttered a sound since we set off. His face was as white as any Seri face can be, a mixture of fear, and I suspect, car sickness, a malady that many Seris suffered in those days before they owned their own vehicles and were accustomed to riding. By contrast, Capitán's normal, rich brown color was returning and his screams were fewer and less intense. Either the antivenin was doing its job or he was old enough to withstand the effects of the toxin. Or, on the other hand, maybe the whole thing had been exaggerated to begin with.

Reaching the pavement at Kino Bay we raced the final thirty-five miles to Calle Doce, not a prudent policy in a country noted for its macho drivers, unsafe roads and broken down vehicles. A common practice in Mexico, where the roads are typically banked high above the surrounding terrain, is to make repairs on a disabled vehicle right on the pavement. Since most older vehicles have no hazard lights, this creates great danger. Furthermore, few have functioning parking brakes, so the driver places rocks behind and in front of the vehicle's wheels to keep it from rolling. When the repair is done, the driver usually removes only the rocks restraining the front wheels, leaving those behind the rear wheels as a terrible road hazard for the next driver who comes along.

Capitán slowly became calm and for the last few miles we began to talk—about people, fishing, plants, gringos and scorpions. He even smiled a couple of times between the diminishing convulsions, when I teased him about having been stung by a giant scorpion. Campuzano also began to talk, describing injuries other Seris had received and some he had experienced himself. (In 1973 he was to suffer a serious injury when a fishhook caught him and produced a severe tear. He required major surgery.) During the conversation I watched Capitán intently. It was now evident the crisis was over and he would recover. The trip to the clinic seemed anticlimatic.

Soon the shacks of Calle Doce came into view and we could see the medical clinic, the largest building in town. Capitán began to whimper, fearing the pain associated with doctors even more than he feared the sting of the scorpion. Adolfo and I remained in the Land Rover while Amalia and Campuzano ushered the child into the clinic. They didn't ask me to accompany them, possibly because a visit to a doctor is, for a Seri, an almost embarrassingly intimate occasion.

Adolfo and I settled down for a long wait. I had had enough experience with Mexican clinics to know that patients are many and doctors are few. Fortunately, Adolfo is an uncommonly good conversationalist, a real "good ol' boy." A rather lazy man, he does not carve, although he often sells carvings Amalia has made. He has found he can avoid a lot of work by spinning yarns and feeding gringos information about the way things were with the Seris in the old days. He patiently and willingly answered my unending questions about him and his people, knowing it would put me in his debt. Much of the time was spent laughing.

After a wait of only an hour of so, Campuzano and Amalia emerged with Capitán. They were smiling broadly. Capitán was fine, a captivating twinkle in his dark eyes. The doctor hadn't given him another injection. (This was surprising. In those days Mexican doctors had a tendency to inject a patient on the principle that the patient will feel cheated if not injected.)

The return drive to Desemboque was agonizingly slow. I was terribly worried about my family, who often used the Land Rover for shade, or attached a canopy to it for shade as a ramada. Of course I tried unsuccessfully to mimic the Seris' stoicism, noting that Campuzano was so relieved he appeared to be hypnotized, a phenomenon I have seen with other Seris, leading me to believe that perhaps they can sleep with their eyes open.

When we reached Punta Chueca it was clear I would commit a faux pas if we did not stop. Although I was concerned about my family and the Seris in Desemboque who feared that Capitán was dead there was no emergency to use as an excuse for not stopping. Therefore, we had to stop for a while to spread the news and permit the exchange of gossip and trading of goods that always seems to occur when Seris meet.

We left Punta Chueca enriched by a number of carvings, some amorphous bundles of things wrapped in old Seri skirts, a few dishes, two transistor radios and three additional Indians.

Adolfo was as complacent as ever, cracking an occasional joke, asking me several times to stop so he could relieve himself and trying out on me new schemes whereby he could enrich himself without having to do any work. Amalia, still comforting Capitán, was enthusiastic about conversation, having replenished her supply of gossip from Punta Chueca. She chattered animatedly, her crossed eyes glistening with excitement as she told me how a government official opposed to the Seris' receiving title to Isla Tiburón was reported to have been removed and replaced by a new man who took the side of the Seris.

My passengers now numbered eight, making the interior of the Rover feel like the Black Hole of Calcutta. The drive from Desemboque to Punta Chueca normally took two hours; I had done it earlier in the day in about an hour and twenty minutes. As it was now after noon, I would be somewhat more considerate. Only the tropical roof kept us from being baked alive.

As the heat increased I cursed my lack of foresight. I had gone off without water. The Seris had brought some, of course, but their water is not purified and a few suffer from tuberculosis. Coca-Cola was also available, but it was not mine and warm. Coke, I have always maintained, increases rather than decreases thirst. Mexican coke, with more sugar, is even worse. If I didn't want to die of thirst, I would have to drink out of the Seris' containers. I was so neurotically skittish I thought I could even taste the amoeba in the water and feel the TB bacilli going down, but the water was wet and decently cool.

Capitán, finally relaxed after his ordeal, was sound asleep as we drove into the village. I considered honking the horn as we drove through the town, but thought better of it when I recalled that such action had been used to announce the death of one of the older Seris only a year earlier. I didn't want to give anybody in the Astorga family a heart attack by creating the wrong impression. Then Adolfo turned to me "Daveed, toca el claxón!" (Honk your horn.) I pushed the button. Nothing. The horn was dead. My precautions had become moot.

I had a happy crew in the Land Rover. All were looking forward to spreading the good news. The whole Astorga clan, joined now by Campuzano's relatives, a total of thirty or so, were waiting at José's house. Aurora, Capitán's mother, who looked as though she had aged ten years since morning, looked up from her carving to see Capitán's face at the window. Barely managing to keep from crying, she rushed over and hugged him as he jumped from the Rover, a most blatant public display of affection for a Seri. The ordeal was over.

Patsy said it had been a miserable day, hot, still and gloomy. She had stayed with the children in the shade of a tamarisk tree at José's house, now and then going over to walk along the beach, but she felt helpless and anxious and wished she could talk to the people and console the family. If the Land Rover had been there they would have driven up the coast and gone swimming to cool off. I felt bad about having left them when the heat was such a problem. Yet she was an amazingly good sport and did not complain. As it turned out, the heat was a greater threat to Suzannah than the scorpion had been to Capitán.

We sat in the shade and talked, waiting for the late afternoon hours that compensate by their beauty and coolness for the inhuman heat of the day. Sundown came and we ate, the children playing by the tent, the waves lapping gently on the shore only thirty feet away. In the background we could hear the murmur of voices, the shouts of children, and the eternal clink of metal on ironwood as the relentless work of imitating nature was carried on by untrained but immensely talented artists. As darkness settled over the village, we tucked Suzannah into her scorpion-proof crib, ever so careful that all entry routes whereby the fiends might enter were sealed. Then we crawled into our tent, zipped up the netting and let the eternal sounds of the desert, the sea and the gentle people who understand both so well, lull us to sleep.

Early the next morning Campuzano appeared at our ramada—actually his ramada—which he was allowing us to live in for a while. (We soon learned why. It was at the edge of town and when the wind blew from the desert, the prevailing direction, it was evident the nearby bushes had served as an outhouse for many years.) He presented me with a lovely ironwood figurine carved in the shape of a woman. It was his "payment" to me for my services. Not another word was said.

Capitán now goes by his Spanish name, Salvador. He is handsome, arrogant and proud, just like his father, but will need to develop many talents to equal those of his father. He is attracted to Mexican women, but in other ways is deeply conservative. Salvador seems to resent the story we tell about the scorpion sting, but even he, aloof and haughty, condescends to let me stop by the family hut and chat. And he did take a long ride on my mountain bicycle when I stopped by his home one evening in 1987 when he was 25. He even conceded it was fun to ride.

Since that time I have had a good relationship with Aurora. She has an artistic temperament and is a shrewd business operator, but she is also a marvelous person. A bit brusque, she is generally recognized as one of the best ironwood carvers. We always have plenty to talk and joke about, even as we discuss the price of whatever carving she has for sale.

Antivenin for the sting of a scorpion is now much more readily available, as are disposable hypodermic syringes. The latter are especially important, since the old, reusable types were not only the source of dangerous infections but were painful to the recipient of the injection as well.

A majority of the Seris now live in cement block or pre-cast concrete houses provided by the government. While these dwellings are hotter in the summer and colder in the winter than the old shacks and huts, they do not provide nearly as comfortable an environment for the scorpion as did the old type of residence. The threats to children of death by scorpion sting have thus been greatly reduced. Today the threats come in the form of poor diet, automobile accidents, or alcohol and drug-induced problems that seem in the mid-1980s to be on the increase. I'm not sure if things have improved.

Torote

There were both advantages (mobility) and disadvantages (having to serve as ambulance service) to having one of the few vehicles in town. But as a trader I wanted to curry favor with the artists from whom I purchased artwork and know as much about my wares as possible. A group of women approached me in the spring of 1970 wondering if I might take them on a trip to the hills for necessary materials with which to make their baskets. The request came when I had ample time and I jumped at the chance to take off into the desert.

Basket making is hard work. So many hours are spent in obtaining and preparing the required materials, in addition to the weaving, that production of a basket from start to finish may require more than six months. Completion of the giant, ceremonial basket called the *sappiim* may take more than a year. But the finished product is often a marvel of human creativity and there is general agreement among authorities on handmade baskets that Seri creations are some of the best in the world.

Fortunately, basket making is a social activity. The women, for only women weave, must concentrate on their work, but not to such an extent that they cannot exchange gossip and participate in the running of the household while working. A woman working on an average sized basket can easily set aside her work to be resumed later. With the sappiim, however, intermittent work is less easy. These leviathans, up to four feet high and five feet in diameter, must be covered with large blankets to prevent dirt and insects from penetrating the basket material and a lot of set-up time is necessary before work on them can recommence. While the weavers take great pains to keep their creations clean, extra precautions are taken with the big baskets. Women have sometimes found several weeks of labor destroyed by weevils which eat the basket material. Some have found their work indelibly soiled by dirt.

I was once baffled by a harsh grating noise coming from the Seri baskets that I had in my living room. It took me several days to figure out that a weevil inside one of the coils was casually eating its way around the basket. When I finally extracted the beast, I found it was a full three-fourths of an inch long and had left a couple of huge holes in my museum showpiece. From that time on whenever I purchased a basket, I obtained large plastic bags, placed the baskets inside and sprayed with the most virulent insecticide I could find. Then I sealed the bags off for a couple of days. So much for my commitment to live without pesticides!

Basket weavers are also responsible for the perpetuation of knowledge of the countryside and the use of desert materials in the Seri culture. The gathering of the fiber and the dye materials requires that weavers spend considerable time in the desert. Baskets are made from a desert bush called limber bush *(Jatropha cuneata)* or *torote* in Spanish. This scrubby plant sends out several stalks up to three feet long, which radiate from the ground and are covered with black bark. The branches generally have bright green leaves, especially after rain, but not enough to interfere with harvesting. Torote is usually gathered by the weavers themselves. Numerous taboos surround the harvesting of stalks, one being that they cannot be gathered by an unmarried woman lest her first child be a breech birth, but this prohibition has been less strictly observed in recent years.

Most of the desirable straight-grained bushes in the vicinity of Desemboque have been harvested and the women must venture into the monte or bush to find suitable stalks. Fortunately, torote is plentiful and rejuvenates and grows back after cutting, although not rapidly enough to maintain a sufficient supply near the village. Its abundance insures an adequate quantity as long as Mexican bulldozers do not denude the hillsides and flatlands. The bush is not palatable to livestock and, mercifully, they leave it alone.

Gathering torote is a festive occasion. The women and children and an occasional man, including gullible gringos, seem to relish these expeditions, which give them a chance to get out of town and see what is going on in the wilderness.

Preparation for an expedition often takes quite some time. First, the cutter must wear old skirts and blouses (or old trousers if the cutter is a male), for the fresh sap from the torote contains a powerful red staining agent that leaves indelible marks on everything it touches. These old clothes are taken to the monte and donned over everyday costumes for protection against the dye.

Provisions for food and drink must also be made. A squashed loaf of Bimbo bread (Mexico's Wonderbread), a couple of cans of Vienna sausages, a few pieces of Seri fry bread or tortillas and a plastic bottle of water along with a selection of super-sweet soft drinks will be the noon meal. Not gourmet victuals, but definitely Seri.

The decision must then be made as to where to go. This most difficult part of the preparation often involves protracted discussions. I suspect the Seris believe that torote from different locations has different properties, perhaps both spiritual as well as physical. It is at times like these I envy the three or four outsiders who speak Seri. I have mastered numbers, a respectable number of nouns and adjectives and a smattering of verbs, but the syntax eludes me. I often wish I had a few years to learn the Seri language just so I could understand the women's discussions. I only surmise that the talk centered on the various locations, the quality of the stalks, road access and the abundance of long vs. short stalks. At any rate the discussions lasted half an hour, with all the seriousness of preparation for war.

When preparations had been completed, nine or ten people packed into the Land Rover and we bounced off through the coastal sandy lowlands, over a couple of hills and up the dry bed of the Río San Ignacio toward Pozo Coyote, about eight miles to the north.

It was a warm, pleasant day on the Sea of Cortez, after a chilly night, with a slight breeze and the desert blooming from the winter rains which had been abundant that year. No one seemed concerned about anything in particular. The atmosphere in the Land Rover was one of a picnic. From time to time one of the women would ask me to stop, at least I think that is what she asked me, since, as is the case with most Seri women, she could not or would not speak Spanish. I would stop, another discussion would take place among my passengers, someone would give the word and we would lurch ahead. It had to be uncomfortable for some of my riders, since the Land Rover had only seven seats and the shock absorbers were for decoration only. Those sitting on the floor must have taken quite a pounding and I was apprehensive since car sickness often strikes those who haven't ridden much in automobiles.

We passed the small ranch house at Pozo Coyote and its well of potable water, a small farm and several trees, continued north a few miles and stopped when one of the women uttered my name. The area they had chosen must have given signs of being optimal for the collection of torote. In addition to the torote, there were saguaro, elephant trees, organ pipes, ocotillo trees, creosote and an abundance of the giant cardón, along with dozens of other desert plants which make this part of the Gulf a botanist's paradise.

We split into several groups, according to families, and struck out across the desert. Although I offered to cut torote, I apparently did not inspire confidence. It takes a more practiced eye than mine to determine the proper length, thickness and grain of the stalks for weaving.

Instead, they asked me to help gather *csipx*, a strange lac found only on the stems of creosote bushes in areas where ants abound. Carvers used csipx as a filler for pock marks and cracks in the dense grain of ironwood and as a glue when the brittle wood could not sustain the force of a blow and a carving would fracture. Csipx has since been replaced by synthetic glues that are easier to find, more effective and more reliable.

The application of csipx was an art in itself. The carver would put a knife in the fire until it was very hot and drop a chunk of csipx on the blade. The lac would smoke and soften and the artist would immediately apply it to the surface to be repaired. Nowadays a tube of glue is produced and the repair is made quickly. And efficiently. The Seris gather csipx only when they run out of glue or gringos to provide them with glue. Then, once again they must resort to their ethnobotanical reservoir and harvest csipx.

I was also permitted to join the children in gathering dead trunks of cholla, the kind popular years ago in the Southwest for making artsy lamps. Over the centuries the Seris have discovered that roasting torote to remove the bark, an operation necessary to expose the inner stalk used for weaving, requires a temperature within certain extremes. If the temperature is not hot enough, the tough bark will not be roasted and will be impossible to remove. Cholla seems best to provide the required range of heat. As nasty as it may be with its vicious spines, cholla has its niche in the Seris' life.

Angelita Morales collecting torote

As we wandered around, the women gathering torote and the children and I picking up cholla and csipx, a jackrabbit sprang out of a clump of bushes and darted away. With incredible quickness, one of the girls, Rosamalia Barnet, grabbed a rock and with unerring accuracy hurled it, striking the unlucky beast in the head and dropping it in its tracks. She then walked calmly over to it, hoisted it by its huge back feet and carried it to the Land Rover. When we returned to the village later, she prepared and cooked it for her family. The Seris say that jackrabbit is safe to eat in the cooler months of the year, when it is not infested with tularemia. They never eat cottontail rabbit.

Since that day I have been very respectful to Rosamalia the Rabbit-Killer. She still has a reputation as being a dead shot with a rock. Many errant dogs have discovered to their detriment her prowess with projectiles. Any woman who can kill a jackrabbit with a stone is a good person to have on your side.

After a few hours the women had gathered enough torote to fill up the rack on the Rover's roof. The quality must have been quite good because the fat bundles, carefully tied and bound with strips of ripped cloth, were placed on the roof rack with great care.

There was no sharing of torote, only a comparing of quantities, flexibility and lengths. The Seri culture is individualistic and sharing is a recent concept. For centuries they have lived a hand-to-mouth existence and loaning and sharing are rare unless specific contracts are agreed upon. While there is an elaborate system of giving within an extended family, outside of the family every favor implies a credit to the bestower of the favor and a debit to the receiver.

By this time the sodas were all drunk, the dubious food gone and the children weary and ready to return to Desemboque. We had collected a large pile of dead cholla and I was proud of the ounce or so of csipx I had managed to scrape off creosote branches, much as an opium harvester scrapes off sap from the poppy.

I distributed the csipx and the cholla as best I could among the women, not succeeding very well in making an equitable division, judging from the sullen looks directed at me. Fortunately, I have found the Seris, although sometimes quick to anger, are equally quick to forgive and they have a hard time going for long without laughing. My failure to receive an enthusiastic endorsement for my egalitarian distribution of the csipx was forgotten five minutes later. I figure that a lot of the apparent anger expressed must be for social consumption.

Back in the village I delivered my load of Seris to their huts. The last passenger was Carmalita Burgos, an unmarried, almost thirty-year old woman, who was accompanied by her son. Carmalita was known as an excellent basket weaver. Realizing I might never get a better chance to observe the whole basket-making process, I asked if I might watch her make a basket from scratch. Carmalita knew I would not be photographing her, as I am not much of a photographer and almost never carried a camera with me, so she was perplexed at my request.

Staring at me as though I were daft, she gradually broke into a lovely smile and said "Aahssah," the Seri affirmation. She was delighted to be able to show off.

The next few hours were taken up in preparing the basket materials. First Carmalita built a fire, using some of the cholla I offered her. She carefully roasted the stalks, expertly removing them from the heat at the right time so the bark would slide off. After she peeled the bark from the cooled branches, she took one end in her teeth and bit down, then drew the rest of the branch away from her. The result was a long peeled strip of material from the branch. She repeated this operation until the whole branch had been split into strips.

Watching Carmalita tear the torote into strips made my teeth and jaws ache. She created several piles of strips, each of a different size and from a different part of the stalk, to be used later to perform a specific function. She then tied the longer strips into a coil, making it easier to soak them in water for softening and dyeing.

Carmalita, like most Seris, has enormously powerful teeth and jaws. While partially due to the fluorides occuring naturally in their water and the primitive diet most of them were raised on, I think the women must either develop strong dentition or lose their teeth, for the work of stripping the branches into small pieces is very wearing.

Several women have actually worn their teeth down until they look like sheep's teeth with little more than a few millimeters of enamel protruding from the gums. In the last couple of decades, the Seri diet has become laden with refined sugars and starches, with an accompanying deterioration of their teeth. Yet those women in their middle years or older, mainly those born before 1950 or thereabouts, seem still to have pretty tough enamel.

While I have never observed the production of dyes, it is also an elaborate chore. Seri baskets have two colors in addition to the straw color of the torote—a rich, burnt red and a black. Both dyes are made from bushes which abound in the area. The red dye stains brilliantly and indelibly, which is fortunate, for any lesser dye would soon bleach out in the dry, salty air to which a basket is exposed for the months required for its production. Numerous Seri baskets more than fifty years old still have vibrant, red colors.

Carmalita used a deer bone sharpened to make an awl, the basic weaving tool of basket makers. From time to time the weavers will strike the edge of the basket with the awl, producing a resounding thud, a sound etched in my mind as surely as the sound of ironwood being struck with a machete. As the deer-bone awl pushes the torote through the basket, it makes a distinct squeak as though something needs to be oiled. Another characteristic sound of the Seri village.

I describe these preparations as though they were done consecutively and easily. Actually, they were carried out over a period of two days and involved hours of what I would consider tedious labor. Just when I thought Carmalita was going to start making the tight center coil that is the basis for the basket, she quit. I tried to find out what was going on.

"Carmalita, aren't you going to make the basket now?"

"Saate." (No.)

"Will you begin it tomorrow?"

"Aahssah." (Yes.)

But she didn't begin it the next day, either. We repeated the conversation. Since I had to leave the following day I was becoming a little exasperated. Then I remembered she was teaching me a lot about making a basket and about Seri life—a fair trade. She had no real reason to schedule her work to accommodate me.

"Carmalita, when are you going to start the basket?"

Carmalita looked at me and smiled a tolerant, teasing smile. She was saying, in effect, I will start it when I am ready to start it. You can wait, silly boy.

A month later, while on another visit, I got the basket. It was a tightly woven tray-shaped container fifteen inches across, with about ten stitches and three coils to the inch. The red and black formed a complex Escher-like design radiating from the center toward the edges, giving the appearance of a colorful pinwheel.

I tried to conceal my pleasure, not wanting her to inflate the price wildly, knowing I was a pushover. I needn't have bothered. I could no more fool her than I could weave the basket.

"How much is it?" I hoped for 150 pesos ($12).

"Pesh iansh cansh capjka" (300 pesos). Her smile had a touch of triumph in it.

I hesitated, then handed over the money. She confidently folded the money into her kerchief, smiled coyly at me and walked away.

Flight

The experience of being delivered to Kino Bay in Campuzano's boat on that lovely spring day in 1971 was exciting, but travel by sea through the Seri country was not my usual style. For several years, I made regular trips to Desemboque. My stated reason was to purchase carvings and baskets for resale in the U.S. Ironwood carving was just becoming established then, after its introduction by José Astorga, and word was gradually spreading into the outside world that the Seris could do marvelous things with chunks of ironwood.

But my real reason for frequent visits was that I was drawn to the Seri country and culture and vowed to spend every minute that I could with the Seris, learning their customs, their language, their land and their individual personalities. The purchase of carvings for resale in Tucson was my means of financing the trips. I had to sell a lot of carvings, baskets and necklaces to pay for all the trips I made, so I developed a vigorous little business.

Once or twice a month I made the long journey down from Tucson or Mesa, Arizona, through an unpopulated country on a road with no name. South by dirt road the Rover would journey from Sasabe, Arizona to Altar, Sonora, then west on a paved road to Pitiquito, where a lovely Kino mission is found along with the last available gasoline station. Then I would wend my way south again over primitive dirt roads for the remaining 100 miles, navigating only by isolated ranches with exotic names: Bámori (a Tohono O'odham name), La Ciénaga (The Swamp), El Porvenir (The Future), La Gloria (The Glory), Los Cielos (The Heavens), Los Pozos (The Wells), Las Estrellas (The Stars) and finally Pozo Coyote (Coyote Well). My Land Rover became a familiar sight to ranch hands who worked the range and raised cattle for absentee landholders from Caborca and Hermosillo.

Often I would stop and chat with these true cowboys, who spent most of their life on horseback, as I amassed details on range conditions and personal situations. Gradually the dreadful overgrazing almost universal in Mexico has taken its toll and one by one the little ranch houses have become deserted. The families who once lived there, rendered destitute by a land so abused that it withholds its wealth from those who live on it, providing a return only for the owners, must flee to the cities, in what is almost certainly a vain search for work. Some ranchers knew of the Seris, and some even envied the Seris' rumored affluence, an astonishing irony in lieu of the traditional image of Seris as poor and primitive. Over the decades, other ranchers have become friends with some of the Seris.

On one trip I halted briefly at one of the ranch houses, just to say "Hi" to the man and woman who lived there. He was gone, searching for work his wife said, but, I suspected, never to return. He had left his wife and two children, waiting for the landlord from Caborca to send food that probably would never arrive. She pleaded with me to get word to him that they had no food. I left what I could with her and told her neighbors at the next ranch of the poor woman's plight. These people were not much better off themselves. Today the ranches are largely deserted, a sad end to a tense social drama. Mexico's future will be a battle for peace and bread.

Land Rovers were never designed for comfort and the trip to Desemboque is an exhausting one. The road is bad at best and at its worst is a nightmare of gullies, rocks and sand. On those occasions when my family accompanied me, they would dread the last forty miles or so when my patience was at an end and my familiarity with the road gave me the idea I could drive much faster than was prudent.

But the long trip was worth it all. Arrival was always a thrill, a time tinged with ancient feelings of homecoming. The Gulf suddenly comes into view from a point only a few miles away, and from there I could smell salt air and the sweet scent of arid plants where the desert meets the sea. The town carries the crisp aroma of ironwood smoke. Always, an excited crowd of Seris gathered around the Rover to see what we had brought and who was with us. And always the Astorgas would be there, smiling, excited, knowing I came bearing gifts. Even José seemed to be glad I was there to listen to his tales and pay top dollar for his carvings.

By then, the Seris were beginning to realize their carvings and baskets were highly marketable items. They also noticed that gringos had access to consumer goods unavailable to them. As I left each time, people would ask me to bring things for them on the next trip—cloth, tools, transistor radios, automobile parts, cooking utensils. A man once asked me to bring him a television set, another a large amplifier for an electric guitar.

Most of the smaller requests I was quite willing to honor, because I knew the quality I could provide far exceeded anything they could obtain in Mexico. I said no to the television. Reception is nonexistent there and electricity only sporadic. I hesitated on the amplifier, it would have cost several hundred dollars and I doubted I could make that up in trade. I was somewhat reluctant to comply with another request. I should have listened to my inner voice, because that one order was to bring me a good deal of trouble.

Campuzano was not only an expert fisherman, he was a hunter; only a few deer, poached, of course, but many jackrabbits and even a javelina or two were among his trophies. One day he brought me his rifle—an old .22 caliber he had received years ago as a gift from a North American. The firing pin was broken and he needed the rifle to provide food. Would I get it fixed for him?

Red flags or celestial warnings should have gone off, but I felt only a slight uneasiness. Of course, I said, I would take it to a gunsmith in Tucson and get it fixed. I put the rifle under the seat of the Rover and left for Tucson. U.S. officials do not object to bringing firearms into the country, at least they didn't in those years.

The gunsmith couldn't fix it. He said it would have to be sent to the factory. So how do you do that? Well, he said, it's tricky. It is illegal to send firearms through the mail, so it would need to be shipped by rail, which requires special packing, and would cost at least twenty dollars to ship and probably take six months to repair. Well, good lord, I could buy Campuzano a new rifle, a nice semi-automatic Ruger, for only about fifty dollars, so what the heck. I had never been checked by Mexican officials at the Sasabe border and Campuzano would love the new rifle.

Indeed he did. He was ecstatic about it and didn't mind telling other Seris that "Daveed" had gotten it for him. It wasn't long before another hunter, Manuelito, asked me to bring him one, along with some ammunition. Well, all right, I thought, but this is the last one. I wasn't going into the business of exporting arms to Latin America. The next trip Manuelito had his rifle and bullets (many years later he still had the rifle) and I was apparently up to my ears in trouble.

I'm still not sure how it all happened. Two weeks later, on another trip, I was happily wandering around the streets of Desemboque, watching progress on carvings I had ordered, chewing the fat with some old timers, teasing the young Seri women, and trying to improve my limited mastery of a few Seri words. I walked by the missionaries' house. Becky Moser was at the door.

"David, we need to talk to you."

"Fine. What's up?"

"Come inside."

I did. Becky and Ed's faces were grave. They had heard reports that Mexican police were about to come to Desemboque looking for me because I had been bringing guns to the Indians, a serious crime in Mexico.

Were they positive? Who had told them? They couldn't say for sure, but they were afraid the report was true. They feared for my safety, saying I should leave immediately.

I had heard many reports about the justice system in Mexico and the conditions in Mexican jails, so I needed no further urging. I rushed over to the Astorga's where I had camped, told them what the Mosers had said and began to throw my things into the Rover. I then made a quick trip around town to pick up finished carvings and to plead with the artists not to sell the ones that weren't. I would be back, I promised, but I couldn't say when.

José Astorga was angry when I left

The Astorgas were angry. The missionaries had done it, José said. I shouldn't believe it at all. Those missionaries were not Seris and couldn't be trusted. No one was coming. I should stay there. I would be safe. When the Mosers came over to check up on me, José shook his fist at them. Becky and Ed retreated, looking confused and hurt. Hard feelings remain to this day.

I told the thirty or so people who had gathered that I had to leave, that I couldn't take any chances with the police. I choked back a few tears, fearing this might be my last trip. Luisa and Olga were openly weeping. Several other groups of Seris were discussing the issue heatedly as I jumped in the Rover and shot out of town.

The drive from Desemboque to Sasabe, Arizona on the Mexican/U.S. border normally took me six hours. I had to do it a lot faster than that. As I drove north I was sure I would be apprehended because my well-known Land Rover was a sitting duck. My only hope lay in speed because I knew communications among the Mexican law enforcement people were still primitive, at least in the deserts of Sonora. But, then, so were their methods. They were known to shoot first and advise prisoners of their rights later.

At every turn I expected to meet a Mexican police Jeep or army truck. Desemboque is under the jurisdiction of the police of Caborca, which lies in the direction in which I was travelling, and any emissaries of the law sent from Caborca would likely be on the same road I was taking. Surely, they would be waiting for me at La Ciénaga, the only settlement on my way. But no, of course not. I tried to convince myself that even the police don't know where La Ciénaga is, and if they did, they would not want to drive all the way there just to apprehend a gringo gun-runner.

But how, I thought, could I possibly get past Pitiquito without getting caught? I had seen police cars in Pitiquito and feared they would be lying in wait, for Pitiquito is only a few miles from Caborca. The hour and a half from La Ciénaga was tense. I tried to figure out a way to get through via back streets, but it was impossible. There is only one road through the town and I would have to take it.

The streets of Pitiquito proved to be quiet and indifferent as always. It was dusk as I whipped out onto Mexico 2, the highway that leads to Altar. There was no traffic and only thirteen miles of pavement before I could turn off on to the safer dirt road. Then, passing over the only hill on that stretch, I saw a police car coming in my direction, its red light flashing. That was a sight I had never before experienced in Sonora. I knew I was caught. My heart exploded and I felt my pulse in my throat. The car approached and passed. I recovered quickly as I watched the flashing light of authority fade into the distance in my rear view mirror. I slowed down and caught my breath.

Surely they would catch me when I turned off the pavement at Altar, I thought. It was almost dark and the police would be even more brutal. So far I had just been lucky. At the turnoff at Altar there was nothing. I sped into the night, thankful for the cover of darkness.

But now I had ample time to worry about Sasabe, for the 62 miles of dirt road from Altar to Sasabe is an interminable drive. Not a bad road, but nothing to see. Plenty of time to dwell on one's sins and the inevitable recompense. I felt certain the authorities had closed the border at Sasabe and were waiting to arrest me. I would crash the gate, dragging the fence with me as my macho Land Rover piloted me to the safety of the American flag. No, I mused, they would capture me at the outskirts of Sasabe, not allowing me to get close to the American side.

I passed only two trucks on the whole lengthy stretch. I pulled into the outskirts of the Sonoran side of Sasabe. Nothing. It was pitch black and only a few lights were lit. Two miles to the border and the final confrontation, the unavoidable detention, a night in the Sasabe jail, then transfer—after the usual beatings and torture—to Caborca, then trial by a kangaroo court after rotting in prison for years, without access to a lawyer. My family would be left to fend for themselves.

With a burst of raw courage I reached the final rise before the border station. There, almost blocking the road, was a pickup, a very official looking pickup with an official-looking sign on the side. I was a goner. I prepared to speed up and crash the border. I slouched down in the driver's seat to avoid the expected spray of machine-gun bullets. I could see the headlines, both terrifying and exciting: "YOUNG AMERICAN GUNNED DOWN AT BORDER."

Just as I was prepared to speed by, ramming the pickup if necessary, the vehicle moved. The sign was the name of a cattle ranch south of Sasabe. At the Mexican station, the border guard waved the automatic pass signal. They didn't even bother to ask for my papers. I was home free.

As I drove over the cattle guard that spans the border, I was sure I heard the "Star-Spangled Banner." I had suddenly become: 1) intensely patriotic; 2) a much more loyal, devout family man; and 3) profoundly religious. Although all three passions were to wear off in the next few hours, they demonstrated a potentiality I had always denied. I was safe. And foolish, for I felt so relieved I sold an ironwood carving to a U.S. customs agent for a ridiculously low price.

I had made the trip in less than five hours. I had escaped the heavy hand of the Mexican police, but maybe José had been right, maybe I had fled for nothing, maybe the whole thing was a hoax and the police couldn't have cared less about me. On the other hand, maybe I had burned my bridges behind me, making myself a fugitive from Mexican authorities. Perhaps through brash, reckless acts I had cut myself off from what seemed my very roots and the people I had come to love.

I drove a few miles north of Sasabe, pulled off onto a side road and camped for the night. At that moment, I feared I could never return safely.

Homecoming

After my flight from imaginary police and my sprint back to the U.S.A., I was safe from harm, but my problems weren't over. I had left not only a number of valuable carvings in Desemboque, but also a tremendous emotional investment. The thought of not being able to return was unbearable.

My response to the situation was to go into a depression which neither my wife nor my children could understand, and in which I made little attempt to communicate. I was morose, nursing my spiritual wounds, immersing myself in my duties as a professor at Arizona State University teaching classes in philosophy, obsessed with the town and people I had been forced to leave.

I lamented to anyone who would listen my misfortunes and my supposed expulsion from the people I so loved. The polluted air, the traffic, the endless horizontal cities of my country, the superficiality of everyday life, all were set in opposition to the noble savages and the paradise in which they lived. I idealized the Seris to the point of ludicrousness. Besides, no self-respecting trader can be intimidated by mere security forces. Traders are the foundation of international finance and as such don't get involved with the police. That's the mythology. The fact was, I was pretty scared.

It was not long, though, before things began to improve. Jim Hills, an early collaborator with me on importing and studying the Seri culture, made a trip and brought back news from Luisa that she thought I would be safe and that her brother Santiago couldn't find any evidence the police were looking for me. He believed I could safely return in a while, a few weeks he suggested.

Then I received a letter from the Mosers. No one had come to the village in any official capacity except for some census-takers. They would keep their eyes and ears open and let me know if they saw or heard anything, but they never wrote me again.

Three weeks after my flight I could stand it no longer. I had a long weekend from my teaching duties. Damn the consequences, I would go back to Desemboque. But how? Since my Land Rover could never be camouflaged, I would readily be identified. It was the size of a small tank and the only one around. Well, all right, I would take a bus. That's easy enough as far as Hermosillo, but how would I get to Kino Bay, sixty-five miles away? And then how in the world would I get to Desemboque when there are only two or three vehicles a day that pass in that direction?

Never mind the details. I was determined to go. I told Patsy about my desperation to return to the Seris, packed a few things in a suitcase (while leaving it almost empty as I planned to buy carvings), grabbed a small knapsack and said good-bye. I walked out the door, headed for the Greyhound Bus Depot. Patsy sadly watched me leave.

Ten hours later I was in a seamy hotel room in Hermosillo trying to sleep, ready to spring into action as soon as dawn arrived. I hadn't slept a wink on the bus as it crawled south from Nogales through the many towns in which it stopped: Imuris, Magdalena, Santa Ana, El Oasis and, finally, Hermosillo, 170 miles south of the border. All I could do was wait. I passed the time easily enough on the bus, striking up conversations with a university student and a priest with whom I discussed the plight of Mexican Indians.

I found out that a bus made a run to Kino Bay once a day. At 5am I was up, worried that I would miss its departure at 8am. The bus would get me into Kino at 10am, leaving me plenty of time to find my way into Seri country to the north. I would try my luck at hitchhiking first, however. With a little luck I could get an early start.

Two hours later I was back at the bus station buying a ticket. I hadn't gotten a ride, just a bunch of insults from local machos who would honk at me and make obscene gestures. (Don't ever be a gringo hitchhiker in those areas of Mexico where nationalist spirits run high.) I would have to wait for the bus.

It seemed an eternity before it rattled up, a derelict antique looking as though it would have to be pushed. It chugged along in a leisurely fashion, stopping frequently to pick up and let off passengers. I stayed on the bus till nearly the end of the line in Kino Bay, where the road heads north to

Punta Chueca. With no vehicles in sight, I set off walking under a bright desert sun. I must have presented a ridiculous sight—a young, suitcase-carrying college professor walking along a desert road to nowhere. Crazy gringos!

Unless you are in high spirits as I was, or are monomaniac, I do not recommend walking from Kino Bay to Punta Chueca. Not only are there twenty-two miles of a very hilly dirt road, but it is usually exceedingly hot and there is nothing, I repeat, nothing but desert in between. After five miles or so I began to hope rather desperately that some sort of vehicle would come along and give me a ride. Frequently I would look behind, praying for a telltale cloud of dust. All I could see was the silent, shimmering desert and a few vultures who followed my progress with lazy patience. Two or three miles later, as my arm began to ache, I cursed my stupidity for bringing a suitcase instead of a backpack.

And so I was most grateful for the ride a rancher gave me to Punta Chueca. He was skeptical when he stopped, wondering just what the hell was going on. He was prudent enough to offer me only the back of his pickup, not the front seat with the air conditioner. When we arrived at Punta Chueca he was careful to drop me off at the outskirts, not wanting to risk drawing the ire of the Seris by depositing this weird baggage with them. In all probability he feared that whatever malady I had was contagious. He certainly couldn't envision himself walking to *his* ranch with a suitcase in hand.

Punta Chueca didn't exactly have a ticker-tape parade prepared for my arrival. I got a few curious looks, a couple of raised eyebrows and several feeble pitches for second-rate ironwood carvings. Just the day before, a busload of senior citizens had been in the village and cleaned out all the better carvings.

But carvings weren't my big interest now. I had to get to Desemboque, forty-five miles north, and get there soon. I had only three days of vacation. I asked one of the storekeepers if he knew of anyone going north.

Somebody had just left, he said. Probably nobody else would go for a couple of days. Did he know anybody who would be willing to drive me there? Nope. Nobody had a vehicle that worked. But I should check with Juan Topete.

That I didn't want to do. Juan was an older Seri, a cousin of José Astorga. He was crotchety and unpredictable. Only recently he had come to Desemboque and when he saw me he had given me a royal tongue-lashing for not visiting Punta Chueca more often. After his stern lecture another young man came up to me and tried to console me. "Don't worry, Daveed. Así es." (He's just like that.) The explanation made me feel better, but right now I didn't want to face him and didn't want to deal with his irascible moods. I also, however, wanted to get to Desemboque in the worst way. I walked up to Juan's hut. He was seated outside, carving.

"Shostah, Juan." (Hello.)

"Shostah, quien es?" (Who are you?)

"Soy David. No me recuerdas?" (I am David. Can't you remember, you old goat?) You were just bad-mouthing me a few weeks ago.

"Aye, Daveed, amigo. Que tal? Que bueno verte! Mucho tiempo que no viene. Pase." (Come in beloved stranger. How nice to see you!)

Something was strange. But, then, as my young friend has said, that's the way Juan is. Juan offered me a dilapidated chair and lapsed into small talk. I had little patience for the pleasantries. I didn't mind being rude.

"Mire, Juan, busco un raite hasta Desemboque." (Look, Juan, I need a ride to Desemboque. Could he help me?)

"Por supuesto, hombre. Te llevo en mi panga." (He would take me in his own boat.) Wonderful. Well, not so wonderful since I knew he didn't have a boat, and he told me in the next breath that he had only enough gasoline to take me to Campo Víboras, less than halfway there. Oh, well, halfway was better than no way. How soon could we leave and which boat would it be?

Juan rose and led me to a boat on the beach. It belonged to another Seri but I humored Juan in his illusion that it was his. Soon two other Seris materialized with gas tanks. I paid them, threw my suitcase aboard and jumped in. One of the others fired up the motor. Some young men pushed us off and we sped out of the harbor into the Infernillo Channel. I rode in the prow lying down, staring into the clear water, watching the bottom of the Gulf whiz by. A few dolphins leaped around us, producing in me a euphoria. I knew I would make it.

After a ride of less than an hour I was in Campo Víboras (Rattlesnake Camp), well named because the vipers abound in the area. Once an important winter camp owing to the abundance of *caguama* (green sea turtle) and *totuava* (sea trout), Campo Víboras is seldom used. The caguama faces extinction from over-harvesting and the vast schools of totuava have disapppeared. Their spawning grounds, the Colorado River delta, have been laced with insecticides and deprived by upstream dams of the required natural flows. Recent flooding along the Colorado has produced flows in the delta once again, but probably only for a short time and not long enough to re-establish the once enormous schools of totuava.

Víboras was an idyllic place to be at that time of year. It consisted of a few huts on a narrow peninsula jutting into the Infernillo Channel. I knew the families there and they were delighted that someone had come by who would chat and buy carvings. I sat on the beach and comfortably conversed with a group of ten Seris who left their leisurely work of carving and basket making to pick up news of the outside world and ask questions about my family, especially my son Chris.

But I still couldn't figure out how the devil I was going to get to Desemboque, twenty-five miles away. In those times, days would go by when not a single vehicle would pass through heading north and I didn't feel up to walking twenty-five miles with a suitcase. It was now almost 5 o'clock in the afternoon and would be dark in another couple of hours. I had no sleeping bag, no blanket, no air mattress and even less hope. While the Seris would have loaned me one of their blankets, the thought of contracting the head lice which abound in their habitations didn't especially appeal to me. Just as things were appearing totally hopeless, one of the Seris pointed inland.

"Aye, Daveed, tienes buena suerte. Hay viene El Teniente Coronel." (You lucky guy, you. Here comes Teniente.)

Jesus Segovia, a congenial Mexican who went by the nickname of Teniente Coronel (Lieutenant Colonel), owned one of several small stores in Desemboque. Every couple of weeks he would take a trip to Hermosillo to replenish his stocks of merchandise. Here he was, returning just in time to give me a ride. I grabbed my suitcase and ran the quarter mile out to the turnoff. I didn't want to take any chances on missing a sure bet.

El Teniente was delighted to see me. Of course I could ride along. He knew my presence in Desemboque meant more business for him. However, his Seri wife and daughter rode in the front with him, requiring me to squeeze myself and my suitcase between a hundred or so cases of soda pop, indescribable quantities of foods and some nameless dry goods stashed in the back of his stake-bed truck. Climbing into the back of the truck, I waved goodbye to the Seris of Campo Víboras. At last I was homeward bound.

All the way to Desemboque I sang songs at the top of my lungs to help dissipate the nervous excitement I felt. El Teniente gave me weird looks through the side mirror and I could see him through the cab window,

María Luisa Astorga

exchanging smiles with his wife; yet he seemed to understand. Mexicans do not share the belief of many Seris that North Americans are uniformly stark, raving mad. They view us as rather rowdy souls, but harmless enough, generally good, and naive and eccentric customers.

The truck lumbered along at an infuriatingly slow pace. El Teniente dared not drive fast over the winding road for fear of damaging his cargo. I was getting squeezed severely and was forced to eat more than my share of dust, but knowing we would arrive soon consoled me. Tepopa Point loomed ahead to the west. We overtook and passed it.

It was dusk when we drove into town. I was sort of hidden in the back of the truck, which suited me fine in case it was not yet safe for my presence to be known. A crowd gathered to talk to El Teniente and find out what merchandise he had brought with him. In the fading light, I climbed discreetly over the staked side of the truck and leaped to the ground. I was sneaking away to find Santiago Astorga when I was spied by the ancient María Antonia. She gave a Seri squeal that brought twenty or more people around to the back of the truck. I was trapped.

The Seris are not an outwardly emotional people. But I was touched and grabbed by more people than I can remember. María Antonia had tears in her eyes and there were huge smiles all around, barely visible in the glow of twilight. The rest were grabbing me, trying to sell me various merchandise. A wayward gringo had returned, undoubtedly bearing large amounts of cash to buy carvings, necklaces and baskets. Prosperity was just around the corner. If I was back, money would flow into the town more regularly and dependably. The town's economy was looking up.

Then a second tide engulfed me. Word had reached the church that I had returned. I trust the Deity will forgive me, but I'm afraid I disrupted the church service that was in progress, disrupted it irrevocably. Some of the Seris figure they can have church services any time at all and such services are sometimes fun to go to if there is nothing else happening (and there usually isn't); but a friendly gringo with bucks in his pocket was much more important.

I experienced all the emotions of a homecoming. There were smiles and laughing, a lot of gentle touches, a constant murmuring of the soft, motherly sounds of female Seri speakers, some harsher male Seri laughter (by now the Seri language sounded musical to me, not gutteral as it had when I first heard it), hesitant nudges from women hoping to sell a carving so they could buy soda that night, numerous questions as to the health of my daughter Suzannah, and many inquiries as to whether I had brought tools and cloth to trade for carvings.

Then the Astorgas, Luisa and Amalia, and soon Santiago and Rosa, called me over to their house where I had a cot and blanket. The dogs wagged their tails, the children ran around excitedly, hoping for gifts. José smiled and asked me for a loan of 200 pesos. Herminia hissed at the dogs and scolded the babies. Rosa asked hopefully if I had brought a battery for her old portable radio.

I smelled the ancient, nostalgic perfume of smoke from ironwood and fish. I was definitely home. To this day I don't know whether or not the Mexican police were after me.

The Keeper of the Faith

Chapo is a deep thinker among deep thinkers, a philosopher, naturalist, anthropologist and guardian of the Seri past. An astute observer and critic of the world around him, he is an example of a man caught between two cultures, the past and the present.

Over the years I have seen Chapo (translated "Shorty") carefully examining plants, rocks and bones, making comparisons, classifying and identifying, evaluating items for their religious, curative or economic value. I have also seen him wandering disconsolately in the desert near Desemboque. I have travelled with him on land and sea, watched him experience North American culture in Tucson, seen the joys and sorrows of his family life, and discussed with him the future of mankind and of the Seris. Of late he has been a leading force in the resurgence of Seri dances and songs.

Chapo Barnet, born about 1936, has been especially successful in understanding the behavior of gringos. He has become more or less expert on the quirks, tastes, desires and general eccentricities of North Americans. He knows our weaknesses (he can extract money with little effort) and our strengths (we love to bring gifts and supply him with his special weakness, peanut butter). He also appears to know or at least suspect, that in North Americans a reservoir is available that can be tapped to help protect him and the Seri tribe.

Chapo believes, I think, that the recent prosperity of the Seris will be their ultimate downfall. His father is one of the more traditional and conservative older Seris, but Chapo's sons, bright, quick young men, show little interest in following the old ways. Expert boatmen, well trained by their father, they nevertheless know little of outdoor lore and exhibit less interest in learning. Their predilections lie more in the direction of cars and drugs. It was a comic sight in the early 1980s to see Chapo's eldest son rodding around the streets of Punta Chueca (pop. about 250) in a 1968 Mercury. Punta Chueca has no more than four or five streets, a maximum of two blocks long each. Cruising the "strip" on a lazy afternoon doesn't eat up too much time. Since he probably already had been "promised" to a bride, he couldn't be impressing too many girls rodding through the neighborhoods. In the mid-1980s he was to marry a Mexican girl and move to Mexico City.

The difference between father and sons became clear to me in 1982. I had spent a few days on Isla Tiburón with friends. While poking around our campsite, we discovered the remains of an ancient Seri camp, including many fragments of eggshell pottery, an artifact the Seris ceased to produce many decades ago.

Chapo was scheduled to pick us up, but winds delayed him for a day and he sent his sons on the forty-mile trip instead. When they arrived I mentioned we had found interesting traces of ancient Seris. Where Chapo would have been fascinated and would have investigated the site immediately, his sons paid no attention and showed no desire to climb the small hill to review the site. They were more interested in their stash of marijuana. In the spectacular boat ride back to Punta Chueca, they seemed unmoved by the magnificent scenery. I have made the same trip with their father, who is hypnotized by the majesty of it all (even though he is not above a toke or two of grass himself). He goes out of his way to point out interesting details to the inquisitive onlooker. His sons seemed to pay no attention to such things.

I came to know Chapo under difficult circumstances. His third child (he now has many more) was a lovely daughter. As with all Seri babies, she was born with a shock of jet-black hair, quiet, but alert. Early in her life she became sickly and had one illness after another. In desperation during one illness

Chapo took her to the hospital in Hermosillo where, I was told, she was diagnosed as having spinal meningitis. The attack left her with a horrible sore on her back and very restricted in her activities, yet she remained a bright and cheerful child of four.

As the months wore on she became progressively worse. Unfortunately her mother put a lot of confidence in a Mexican practitioner who called herself a nurse. This woman would routinely give ailing Seris her universal cure—a shot of glucose. This remedy, of course, produces a quick feeling of euphoria, but its effects soon abate. The saddest part of this quackery was that the nurse sometimes failed to practice hygienic requirements. She injected Chapo's daughter with either an unsanitary hypodermic syringe or a contaminated solution. The child soon became critically ill.

I was in Desemboque the day after Chapo left to take his daughter to the hospital again. María Marcos, Chapo's wife and Campuzano's sister, stayed behind, as Seri mothers must, to take care of the rest of the family. Since I had business in Hermosillo, I decided to locate Chapo to offer my assistance.

I found him at the hut that served as parsonage for an evangelical preacher who was working among the Seris of Desemboque. The dwelling had become a hostel for Seris visiting Hermosillo. Chapo was there, carrying out a vigil of anguish. His deep brown face was ashen and I knew things were not good for his daughter. How was she? Very grave.

It was late at night. I threw my blanket and petate (a thin mattress woven from reeds) on the floor and tried to sleep. The snoring of several Seris and Mexicans staying at the parsonage for various reasons made sleep difficult. Several times through the night I looked up and saw Chapo, barely visible in the vague illumination, sitting upright on his petate, unable to sleep. I could tell that for some reason Chapo was blaming himself for his daughter's illness.

Early in the morning I offered to drive him to the children's clinic where his daughter was a patient. We were joined there by his sister, Rosamalia the Rabbit-killer, and one of her cousins. On the door was a list of patients and their conditions. Hers was categorized as "very delicate."

She had died during the night and had been left in her crib, her eyes wide open. An attendant stood by as Chapo gently stroked her forehead and closed her eyes. Rosamalia wept softly. The attendant tried to feign sympathy, but she had seen countless children die similar deaths. At that time, life in Mexico was frequently short and miserable and it was clear for this attendant that intense sorrow had long ago been replaced by resignation. After a suitable time she efficiently moved us on and made arrangements for the body to be wrapped and prepared for the return to Desemboque.

Chapo suffered horribly from the child's death. I learned later that he took to heart some of the preaching from the Mexican preachers in Desemboque. Their message was that God hates such barbarian customs as face-painting and dancing and long hair on men and would punish those who committed these abominations. Chapo believed he had been punished for having long hair and dancing the *Pascola*, a traditional Seri dance, which he did exquisitely well.

For several months he lost weight, spoke little and retired from social life. He spent many hours wandering in the desert away from the village. He steadfastly refused to dance any Pascolas or to sing Seri songs. He fished little, carved not at all. His family survived on gifts from relatives and by the little artifacts that his wife María was able to make and sell.

One day, a month or so after the death of his daughter, I met him walking aimlessly in the desert far from the village. I yearned to console him, but felt clumsy and foreign. Nevertheless I tried. "It is very hard, Chapo, I know." I told him. "Yes, Daveed, I am very sad." But as he spoke I felt that Chapo was growing stronger.

Gradually, he recovered. He became more social, went back to carving and spent more time in Punta Chueca where gringos abound. He began to dance the Pascola again. His ability to recall and compose literally dozens of Seri songs made him an invaluable resource for perpetuating Seri culture. He also took up smoking, and not just tobacco either. From time to time he would drink tequila or beer. Most of all, Chapo became a shrewd businessman and an authority on herbs and plants of the Seri desert, many of which he had investigated while mourning the death of his daughter. A decade later Chapo had gained international fame as a Seri dancer. He is a marvelous person.

It was at the time of his return to active Seri life that Chapo decided to accompany several of us gringos on a backpacking trip to Isla Tiburón. The island is off limits to all non-Seris except for those who have influence with the government and during a short hunting season. I fit in neither category, but I was to discover there is an additional circumstance under which permission can be obtained: being accompanied by a Seri. Chapo was a passport.

The island, Ta-e-oak in Seri, holds a spell over the Indians. Almost all Seris over thirty express a nostalgia for life on the island, although few have ever lived there. Most would rather live there than on the mainland, they say.

Why don't they return? I'm not sure, but the lack of Mexican stores and modern conveniences such as soda pop and white bread are among the chief reasons. They also know there would be hassles with the Mexican government, which has decreed that no permanent settlements shall be permitted. But even if they could return, they probably wouldn't. Some realities destroy the beauty of our fantasies.

Chapo is no exception. I have accompanied him to the island three times and it is clear that he views the place with reverence and longing. Chapo's eyes become a little misty when he approaches the island. Or maybe I am reading too much into his complex visage.

In November of 1977 Seri expert and art trader Jim Hills, Bill Hoy, then superintendent of Fort Bowie National Monument, and my brother Dick and I set off for a few days on the island. Chapo was our passport, leader and eager participant.

Chapo did not want to leave his boat unattended while we hiked, so a Mexican boatman ferried us across the Infernillo to the island. We checked in at the marine garrison across from Punta Chueca where the island's only permanent inhabitants are located. The marines patrol the island at times and watch for *contrabandistas* (smugglers) and other potential illegalties. Their stint has to be unpleasant, for the place abounds with jejenes. Their small building provides no screen against the diabolical tormentors and I have seen marines with their torsos literally covered with jején bites.

After a wait of nearly two hours, the federal game official who could give permission for entering the island showed up. After we convinced him that Chapo would accompany us and we were neither hunters nor smugglers, he granted us permission to hike.

Isla Tiburón is formed by two long mountain ranges with an intervening valley and a coastal plain on the eastern side. An area of almost 500 square miles, it is a desert treasure. Because it has never been grazed by livestock, it retains a biota under almost perfect natural conditions. Fortunately the Mexican government has not permitted permanent human habitation on the island, except for Seris whose presence is transient. Mexican fishermen are permitted to camp temporarily at a couple of places, but except for the marines, the island is uninhabited.

Tiburón wildlife is remarkable. Deer and coyote abound, although I believe the mountain lion is absent. Perhaps because of ample forage and lack of large predators, the mule deer grow very heavy and sport massive antlers. My brother Dick and I have found several five-point antlers on the ground where they lay after being shed. The Seris say desert bighorn used to frequent the ridges of the mountain ranges, but a recent attempt by the Mexican government to re-introduce them failed. Some Indians are said to have spied a few bighorn swimming across the channel to the mainland.

Several permanent water sources or *tinajas* well-known to the Seris are found on the Island. The largest ones are considerably inland and are referred to by the Seris as *carrizos*, after a bamboo-like plant that grows in great numbers around the water seeps. It was from carrizo that the Seris used to make their versatile and highly maneuverable balsas, an ability they have lost.

Chapo was eager to hike with us to the carrizo called *Tinaja Anita,* on the east side of the island. He had assured us before we left that it was a good long hike to get there—about ten kilometers, he figured. All the older people from Punta Chueca agreed when we told them where we were going and all pointed out the location of the Sierra Comcaac, one of the two high ranges on the island. There, below a white stratum, was the carrizo. Good water, they assured us.

The Mexican boatman dumped us off an hour later, on the shore of a long bay, perhaps six miles from Punta Chueca. Except for the marines, we were alone on the island. Our destination lay a good four hours ahead. The boatman would pick us up at noon two days later, at least that's what he said. I was cynical due to my numerous disappointments in Mexico. We were on our own.

And so we set off, working our way up the long stretch of flat bajada, the gradual slope to the base of the mountains where we would find the carrizo. The going was easy, but we proceeded slowly, aware that the thick desert grasses, never grazed by livestock, could easily hide a rattlesnake that would be more apparent in the overgrazed lands on the mainland. We hoped the other vegetation would shelter deer, which, judging from the numerous droppings and footpaths, must abound in the area, but we spied only a few.

We made good time the first hour. Jim, Bill, Dick and I had massive, sophisticated backpacks, sleeping bags, stoves and all the convenient, space-age paraphernalia that we drool over in catalogues. Chapo carried a blanket under his arm, a plastic bottle of water and a squashed loaf of ITT's Bimbo bread. As we strolled along, Chapo stopped from time to time to examine various specimens of the lush desert vegetation, patiently explaining to us the intricate secrets of the plants and some of their potential uses.

After another hour, when we were halfway up the bajada, we decided to stop. We set up camp in a small wash, gathered a few armsful of ironwood for a fire and fixed supper. I was suddenly made aware that

Chapo was wearing dress shoes—without any socks. Odd, I thought, but "muy, muy Seri" (very, very Seri). It made my feet hurt just thinking about his hiking all that distance without socks. It didn't surprise me however, for the Seris have lived so much of their lives out of doors and barefoot that they have extremely tough feet. Their village beaches are covered with every conceivable kind of sharp, cutting object so individuals with tender feet would not last very long.

The night was soft, cool and full of wild sounds. It was by no means my first night on the island as I had camped on the beaches several times before. This was my first time inland, though, away from the soothing rhythm of the ocean. Coyotes, owls and other night birds filled the air with their mysterious sounds. I hoped we would not be visited by rattlesnakes of which the island has more than its share—at least three species. Unable to generate warmth themselves, they search out heat sources with great accuracy and have been known to seek the warmth of human bodies on chilly evenings.

I found a hollow in the grass already prepared for me by a deer who had slept there recently, unfolded my pad and sleeping bag and fell asleep, disturbed only briefly by my snoring companions. It was a delicious night. We were alone in a primeval paradise with the nearest human ten miles away.

We were up early in the morning, awed by the number of birds and the beauty of this island wilderness, still mostly free of the smudge and smell of man. We delayed departing due to the heavy dew that had fallen during the night, not wanting to pack our trappings until they were dry. Chapo was mystified by our delay. He had only to roll up his blanket and he was ready. He smiled quizzically at me and I understood. Usually, he must have been thinking, gringos are in a hurry. Now I have to wait on them. Crazy gringos!

Finally we were off. Within an hour we had reached the foot of the Sierra Comcaac which rises 4000 feet above the Gulf of California. Chapo led us up into a canyon. Jim, who had been to the carrizo previously, agreed with Chapo's directions.

Gradually the going got tougher. A mile or so later, Chapo told Jim we needed to turn to the left, scale a side of the canyon and descend into another canyon. Jim at first questioned his directions, then agreed, realizing it is not wise to argue with a Seri about locations while one is in Seri country.

We should be there soon, I hoped. But it was not to be. The canyon was getting steeper, the heat was fierce and our water was running low. The air shimmered as it was heated by the sides of the canyon. The temperature continued to rise as the canyon narrowed and the sun's heat became more concentrated. I drank more and more water and then managed to drop my

Chapo Barnet signing documents granting ejidos to the Seris

canteen, losing most of what was left. Everyone else had drunk most of their water, too. After another mile my pack became unbearably burdensome. Water gone, thirst building, there had better be plenty of water at the carrizo, because I would drink at least two gallons.

Another slow half mile. The going was more difficult. It was necessary to hop from boulder to boulder and ledge to ledge. The sun was almost straight up, bearing down on the canyon's sheer sides. Large, thorny bushes—catclaw, ironwood, mesquite, palo blanco, hackberry—clogged the dry stream bed, catching on our backpacks and making our progress excruciatingly slow. If we didn't get to water soon I was going to be in trouble. Dick's face was flushed and Bill Hoy was the color of cement. Chapo smiled, looked at all of us as a doctor looks at his patients and plodded on.

The canyon turned abruptly to the right. In the dry watercourse were the remains of some algae, a puddle long since dried up. A bad sign—maybe the carrizo would be dry. Then we would have to hike back with no water and there would be no boat for at least a day.

I was so thirsty and tired I decided to drop my pack. I would come back later and pick it up. Bill did the same. Dick, younger and stronger, and Jim, in better condition, managed to keep up with Chapo with their packs on. I brought with me my water bottle and Sierra Club cup, hoping it wouldn't be in vain. Gnats whined in my ears and crawled over my eyes, attracted by the sweat that was pouring from me. Flies buzzed in the still heat.

We continued to labor our way up the canyon. Hotter and hotter. It was November, but the temperature must have been over 100 degrees. Then suddenly in front of us loomed a huge thicket of carrizo, the tall reed grass. Water at last! I rushed through the thicket. No water, just a tiny seep, not deep enough to get a sip from. Panic engulfed me. Bill tried to think of something articulate to say. The carrizo had dried up!

From far above, Jim yelled down to us, "Plenty of water up here." Bill and I staggered up a couple of rock ledges and over some fig tree limbs. In front of us shimmered a pool of clear water three feet deep and fifteen feet across. We were there.

Never did water taste so good and sweet. For half an hour Bill and I stared into the pool, drank, and marveled at the miracle of cool, clear water. Jim and Dick decided to explore further up the canyon. Chapo went off by himself, meditating or studying something about the island. Bill and I took a walk up a side canyon, not wanting any more exertion than necessary. There we found another carrizo, though not one with as much water as the first.

After lunch, Dick and I ventured into a canyon above the carrizo. There we discovered a deep pool in the shape of a bathtub, just meant for a quick dip. In record time we were splashing around, easily forgetting that only a short time ago we were suffering from heat exhaustion and severe thirst. Chapo spent much of the day continuing his botanical explorations. Because the carrizo is an oasis of sorts, it nourishes numerous plant species one would hardly expect to find on a desert island. Chapo was particularly fascinated with the wild fig trees bearing tiny, edible fruits. He gathered and carefully examined several plants unfamiliar to the rest of us. At that point I resolved to take up botany so I could begin to understand Chapo's fascination with plants.

The evening was soft and refreshing as cool air from the higher slopes flowed down the canyon and enveloped us. We sat around the campfire and told tall tales, speaking mostly in Spanish so Chapo could participate. The light flickering on Chapo's face gave him the appearance of an exotic Inca king. He related various tales of the ancient Seris, his theories on gringos and the nature of the universe. When we occasionally lapsed into English, Chapo was able to follow our conversations remarkably well. His studies of gringos included careful attention to our language.

It was when we were preparing our camp for the night that two problems struck us. Camping near the carrizo on the only flat patch of land available (even at the carrizo the canyon was steep, narrow and rocky), we found to our dismay that the jejenes had discovered another habitat to their liking besides the mangrove swamps they inhabit on the coast.

Jejenes are particularly insidious, not only because they are biting, bloodthirsty demons as I have previously pointed out, but they can penetrate ordinary mosquito netting with ease. Also, although their bites seem harmless at first, within twelve hours the swelling increases, accompanied by an itch that seldom disappears in less than four or five days. Jejenes can make any location into a burning hell. The Seris have been most wise to abandon jején-infested areas during the warm months when the bugs are active.

I recall an evening when I had brought my family to the island for an overnighter. We were all safe, we thought, inside a small dome-type tent. Just as we were about to fall asleep we heard the singing of jejenes in our ears, a sound rather higher-pitched than that of a mosquito. Turning on a flashlight we were horrified to find the tent alive with the evil fiends. They had come right through the netting. It was too hot to sleep under blankets, but the minute we removed them we were attacked by the voracious insects. It was a long, miserable night, one whose scars we bore for many days afterwards. After that time I always asked the Seris before camping in an area, "Are there jejenes?"

This time, in order to escape the jejenes, we moved up the canyon wall to an area where there were overhangs and, we hoped, no jejenes.

Fortunately they didn't seem inclined to leave the watered area, for they didn't follow us. Mosquitos were another story, but a huge bonfire in the side of the canyon seemed either to incinerate them or to provide a strong incentive for them to keep their bloodthirsty bodies elsewhere.

Then the second problem struck—the choking smoke of the ironwood. The area in which we proposed to sleep was a semi-cave, an overhanging rock lip that was not particularly well ventilated. It was not an ideal campsite, but it was the only place we could find that approached flatness. I unrolled my sleeping bag and pad and lay down. Within a few seconds I realized that the elimination of the mosquitos had been accomplished at quite a price: the smoke from the smoldering fire was choking me and was killing my asthmatic lungs. Dick, Jim, Bill and Chapo seemed oblivious to the smoke. Or maybe it was the quart of tequila they had drunk that acted as an anaesthetic.

Finally I made a basic, existential decision. I am a very light sleeper and could not possibly sleep under these circumstances. If I were to extinguish the smoking embers, the mosquitos would return. If I didn't, I would asphyxiate in the smoke. I had to leave. My choices were no more palatable than Odysseus' option of Scylla or Charybdis. But a plague of jejenes was preferable to asphyxiation. I opted for the scourge of insects and returned to the canyon bottom. Covering myself with all manner of clothing, I sweated profusely and awakened soaked in clammy garments. But I slept a little and survived with only a dozen or so bites.

My heart still goes out to my hearty comrades who, with iron will and steadfast courage and no more anaesthetic than a bottle of tequila, managed to endure the toxic vapors and potent carcinogens. I guess Chapo was accustomed to sleeping in the company of ironwood smoke. He did fine. The others are due to succumb any day now.

Chapo continually revealed new mysteries to us. On our return to the coast, a hike far more pleasant than our hike in, he introduced us to the fruit of the pitahaya agria *(Stenocereus gummosus),* a sprawling, elongated cactus closely related to the organ pipe, a large cactus found in southwestern Arizona. These fruits abound in the fall on the gulf coast and were especially concentrated on this part of Isla Tiburón.

Pitahayas are delicious. With a taste rather like that of fresh raspberries, they have a juicy texture and refreshing quality matched by no other fruit. They can assuage a thirst better than any other substance I have tasted and their red juice stains better than the most durable Dupont dye. I can also testify that gorging oneself with these delectable fruits is a great way to go. Even if I had not learned so many other things from Chapo, I would immortalize him for introducing me to pitahayas.

The story of our hike must have generated considerable interest among the residents of Punta Chueca and I would love to know what sort of details and descriptions Chapo provided for his audiences. At any rate, enough interest was aroused that the following May, when it was far hotter than it had been on our journey, several young men boated over to the island and hiked up to the carrizo. They made the trip up and back in one day. Barefoot.

Jim Hills has a penchant for ideas that bear wonderful results. A year after we hiked to the carrizo, he and Dick and I decided to hike to another carrizo, this one located on the west side of Isla Tiburón. We went unaccompanied by a Seri, a move of dubious rationality, but necessitated by the circumstances of the moment.

This carrizo, called *Tinaja Sausal*, is a good six miles away from the ocean. The route is less strenuous, however, and an old jeep trail ends not too far from the water. All along the timeworn foot path fragments of pottery indicate that the ancient Seris carried water from the spring to their camp by the ocean. The fragments also suggest that many ollas with their precious liquid were broken and their contents lost to the thirsty soil. It makes me tired just thinking about it. It must have been a real drag to be carrying a few gallons of water in a pot on one's head and stumble upon a rattlesnake!

When we reached the tinaja, we were no less delighted than when we had reached Tinaja Anita. This one had a bit more water and a pool that invited swimming. We lolled around a bit, enjoying the pure water and the desolate magnificence of the scenery. As we were preparing to leave, Jim suggested we fill our containers with spring water so we could take some back to the Seris in Punta Chueca.

We each carried about a gallon those long six miles back to the boat, a work of love if there ever was one. When we returned to Punta Chueca I had forgotten we had the water gift, but Jim hadn't. He presented a large canteen full to Amalia Astorga who was living there at that time with her husband Adolfo.

When she heard that the water was from the Tinaja Sausal, Amalia's eyes lit up and she took a long drink. Then, in rapid-fire Seri, she told all the others around that here was water from the carrizo. Soon a crowd developed, all enjoying the pure, sweet water from their ancestral source. After they had all drunk, she summed up the mood, saying to me in Spanish: "What good friends we have who would bring us sweet water from the carrizo. It is the best water in the world."

Yes, Jim sometimes has strokes of genius.

In the spring of 1973, a couple of years after the death of Chapo's daughter, I visited Desemboque with Jim Riggs, a rancher friend from the Chiricahua Mountains in southern Arizona. Jim wanted more than anything to see some boojum trees *(Fouquieria columnaris),* or cirios, as they are called in Spanish.

This strange but spectacular plant, which in the Seri country grows to a height of more than thirty feet, looks like an inverted turnip with branches only at the top growing parallel to the ground. A relative of the ocotillo (a cactus-like plant common in the southwestern U.S.), the boojum is found only on the slopes of the Sierra Bacha in northwest Sonora just north of Desemboque and in Baja California, where they grow in great profusion. Jim had seen a couple of live specimens at the Arizona-Sonora Desert Museum in Tucson, but he really wanted to see them growing in the wild.

I had made the rough trip to see these boojum trees a couple of times, for a few specimens are accessible by a rough jeep trail that leads north from Desemboque into the Sierra Bacha. However, I didn't have my Land Rover anymore and my Volkswagen Bus couldn't get us closer than a two-hour walk. Instead, I set about finding a Seri who would take us to the boojums by boat. I assumed it would be easy to find someone willing to make an easy few dollars and do some sightseeing at the same time.

The first couple of Indians I approached weren't interested, even if I were to pay them. I upped the price. No dice. Not interested. Then I ran into Chapo on the beach. His interest in nature gives him a scientist's curiosity sufficient to overcome some fears arising from folklore. Would he take us to see the boojums? He thought for a minute and stared out over the ocean. He couldn't take us in his boat he said, but he would try to get a boat and go with us to help find the boojums. I knew Chapo had a boat, but I also knew the complexity of interfamily use of boats, so I didn't think it overly odd that he wouldn't take us himself.

A half hour later we were in a boat. Chapo rode in the prow, the non-too-friendly boatman and a companion rode in the rear and Jim and I sat in the middle. It was about a half hour ride to where the desert hills met the ocean. The Gulf was calm and the going was smooth. As we neared the hills, Chapo pointed to a tiny cove where the boat could land. The Seri boatman buried the prow in the sand and Chapo, Jim and I got out, leaving the other two, who preferred to remain in the boat.

It was a steep climb of a couple hundred yards to the first boojum trees. Chapo led the way and approached the first one with intense interest. Jim shared my wonder at the grotesque plants, marvelling at nature's curious means of adapting a species to a desert environment. Then we saw more plants above us and climbed up to them.

When we reached the next group of boojums, Jim decided to cut off a tiny branch to take back with him. Just as he was making a cut with his knife we heard a sharp whistle from below. The boatmen were waving to us to come back down. While we had been examining the boojums, a sharp wind had sprung up and the boat was rocking. Chapo did not hesitate, saying we should return at once. The Seris respect wind and refuse to take boats out into a strong breeze. It was a good long ride back and they didn't want to take any chances.

We descended quickly and hopped into the boat. The boatman immediately shoved off and we headed back to Desemboque. It was a good thing we left when we did, for the wind picked up rapidly, becoming strong and cold within an hour. If we had waited, we would have had a hard time making it back.

As we walked up the beach afterwards, I asked Chapo about boojums, wondering how encyclopedic his knowledge of them would be.

"Chapo, what can boojums be used for?"

"No se, Daveed." (I don't know.)

"Have you ever used any part of the plant for anything?"

"No, Daveed, that is the first time I have even been close to a boojum."

"Really? The first time? Why?"

"Well, I've never really been close to one because I've never been in the area before."

I accepted his explanation, but it made no sense. Chapo had been everywhere in the Seri country and examined every plant in the whole region. But I had to take him at his word. Before I had an opportunity to ask anymore about boojums it was time for us to leave. We packed our belongings and bid the Seris goodbye.

I did not return to Desemboque for more than five years due to my work. When I did return, the pueblo had changed considerably in appearance. The Mexican government had constructed block houses for most families. They had also built a rock jetty so boats could unload more easily, but the beach shifted and filled in the area around it, leaving it inland and useless. There were more pickup trucks in town, and a new diesel generator provided electricity to most houses for a couple of hours each night, at least when it worked. Oscar Topete's store, washed away in a flash flood a decade ago, had been replaced and expanded.

I walked down the main street, confused by the new facade of the village. Somehow things seemed different, uneasily non-Seri. But soon I heard the familiar sound of ironwood being carved and the happy sounds of children playing along the beach. Nothing had really changed.

On the street I ran into Roberto Herrera (also known as Robert Thomson), a respected elderly Seri who has been a consultant for outsiders studying the Seris. He looked much older and it took him a few moments to recognize me. Then he smiled.

"Aye, Daveed. Mucho tiempo que no vienes. Te hemos echado de menos." (We haven't seen you for a long time. We have missed you.)

I explained that my new work didn't give me as much freedom. He was understanding and sympathetic.

"Roberto, tell me something," I asked. "For years I have wondered about the boojum tree. Is it a special plant?"

"O, si, Daveed." (Yes, it is a special plant indeed.)

"Why is it special?"

"It is a plant of great power. For this reason the Seri people stay away from it."

"And what is its great power?"

Roberto thought for a moment. "You see, Daveed, if you in any way harm it or cut it, a great and dangerous wind will come up and it will bring harm to you. You must not hurt a boojum in any way." He smiled at me, but his smile was serious.

I thought back. Chapo had been courageous to approach the boojums with us. The other Indians refused to go near the plants. As soon as Jim had cut the boojum, a wind had sprung up. The other Indians had been watching us from below and tried to get us away from the boojums before we could harm them. We had been lucky to get back to Desemboque without capsizing.

Roberto took his leave and walked slowly back to his house, his pace slowed by age.

No, I thought, no plant can have such power. It is a superstition, pure and simple. Just a superstition.

Brujo

"You'd better check your tent, Daveed," said Fernando Romero.

"Why is that?"

"Because a big wind just blew into your camp."

I was sitting with Fernando outside his hut in Desemboque, watching the last light from the setting sun. It had been an extraordinary evening that I wished would never end. For some reason everyone was happy. Fernando was sober, his family was chattering gaily and there had been no quarrels in town.

Several of us were camped near the beach a couple of miles north of Desemboque. It was late July, hot and humid. As there were ample gnats and mosquitos about, I had brought a tent. We had come into town to chat and just hang out and enjoy the dusk with the Indians.

It was a good time to be in Seri country. Few tourists would brave the searing heat and ferocious insects of the desert summer and venture up sixty miles of dusty, bumpy, winding road just to get a Seri ironwood sculpture. As a result, there was no hurry among the carvers to produce figurines and everyone was willing to spend a few hours chatting. Even the women who approached us with carvings and necklaces to sell seemed to recognize that the hard sell approach wouldn't work and good-naturedly accepted our lack of interest in normal commerce.

A huge thunderstorm developing in the east had decorated the entire eastern horizon with a spiderweb of lightning so spectacular that Jim Hills had decided to photograph it. The rain never reached us, but a few gusts of wind had blown in and rearranged some things in town. The clouds had then moved over the town and out into the Gulf, creating a sensational sunset with brilliant reds, purples and violets alternating with dark clouds as the sun neared the low mountains on Baja California, some sixty miles away.

A school of dolphins had come somersaulting by, much to our delight. The sun was setting amidst a fiery glow as the storm sent yet more clouds to the horizon, principally for our benefit I concluded, and the ocean reflected a glassy texture, something that usually happens just before a summer storm.

Fernando was a man of such extraordinary powers and talent that I continue to hold him in awe even though I was appalled at his heavy drinking. Earlier that evening he had demonstrated his uncanny abilities. As we sat outside his hut, I noticed that he was staring out toward Tepopa Point, ten miles or so along the beach to the southwest.

"What do you see?" I asked, hoping for more excitement.

"Here comes Salomón," he reported. Salomón had gone fishing earlier and people were eager to see if he would bring back a good catch for supper. Because red meat spoils rapidly in the summer, it was not unusual for there to be long periods when it was not available. By the time the shopkeepers could get such meat to Desemboque to market it, it would be close to rancid. Fresh fish was always most welcome under these circumstances.

I couldn't see anything, but as I watched, a tiny dot materialized on the horizon. That dot was a Seri boat with three fishermen and, everyone hoped, a good load of fish, maybe even a caguama. Fernando continued to watch. I peered into the dusky grey of the evening ocean, trying to catch a better glimpse of the boat. After a few moments he nudged me.

"It's not Salomón, it's Saúl."

Well that was fine too. Saúl had also gone fishing and he could bestow the same bounty on the village as Salomón. But I had no idea how Fernando could tell the difference.

Shortly though he exclaimed, "There's Salomón now," pointing in the same direction. I could still see only one dot but as I peered into the fading light another dot appeared on the horizon.

"How can you tell which is which?" I asked him. After all, I couldn't even tell that the dots were boats much less distinguish between them.

Fernando gave me a flash of his well-known smile.

"Just wait. You'll see."

Ten minutes later I could tell that there were in fact two boats approaching but I still couldn't tell one from the other. In another ten minutes the first boat arrived; it was, of course, Saúl. He was greeted by a crowd of people waiting on the beach, whereupon he threw on the sand a heap of triggerfish, considered a trash fish by North Americans but a delicacy by the Seris, who with good reason enjoy its delicate and delicious but bony flesh.

A few minutes later Salomón arrived, bringing not only more triggerfish, but a few mackeral and a small caguama.

The beach scene when a fish-laden boat arrives is often wild. People crowd around hoping for a goodly portion. Dogs and cats also gather, waiting for the pile of entrails which they will carefully pick over, and large numbers of shore birds linger at a prudent distance. Several men and an occasional woman (from families who have no men) roll up their pant legs or hold up their skirts and walk out a few feet in the water—not far though for fear of stingrays—grab a fish and begin to clean it.

The fish, except for triggerfish (which are smaller and more difficult to clean), are usually cleaned and gutted there on the beach with precision-aimed machetes. The heads of any large fish are distributed to appropriate families and are roasted for the meat and the eyes, quite a delicacy.

At times the fish are sold either to the government-sponsored cooperative—which functions from time to time, but more often than not is in a state of chaos—or to Mexican buyers who keep trucks of ice nearby, and in a leisurely fashion haul their load to Hermosillo.

In summer though, most fishing trips are for fish to be consumed locally and the return of the boats signifies feast or famine. It is not that the Seris will starve in the absence of fish, or, for that matter, in the absence of food sold by the little stores in town. But life can be pretty dull when the diet consists of snails, mesquite beans and cholla fruits.

To this day I cannot explain how any human could have vision so acute as to distinguish, at a distance of several miles, two boats which look the same to an untrained observer at a distance of 200 yards. But that is just one of the remarkable facts about Fernando. He had almost super-human vision.

So when a man with Fernando's faculties warns you to check your camp, you had better check your camp. I found Jim, who had driven me into the village, and we jumped in the truck and sped out to camp. Fernando had been right. My tent was gone—not just blown over, but gone—and without a trace.

Carl Noggle, a physicist and lightning expert who had the fortune to be with us, was a bit dismayed. He had left his large knife and his solid gold wedding ring in the tent. He was not enthusiastic about losing them. Carl got a large flashlight out of the truck and swung the beam around. No sign of the tent, not even a drag mark on the ground indicating the direction in which it might have blown. No people had been around so it could not have been stolen. The air was still—eerily so. The hypothesis that the tent had been blown away seemed incredible.

Then it occurred to him to shine the beam out into the ocean. There about an eighth of a mile out in the Gulf floated my tent. Hopeless. The tide was going out and we had no boat. By the time we could get back to Desemboque and get a Seri boat, even assuming that they would be willing to go out at night, the tent would be lost or sunk. Confound the luck! Fortunately Carl is not easily intimidated by adverse circumstances.

"Let's walk out and get it," he suggested in his calm reassuring voice. "The water won't be deep and the stingrays are gone from the shallows until cold weather."

Well, all right, I answered, although the thought of walking out into the ocean when it was almost pitch black didn't exactly appeal to me. While helping the Seris catch octopus, I have been stung by jellyfish, seen dead sea snakes (which are highly venomous) and been warned about numerous poisonous fish such as the scorpionfish which haunts the bottom and can paralyze with a toxin carried on its fins. It was hard for me to be enthusiastic about walking through their habitat when I couldn't see where I was going.

With the retreating tide the tent was moving farther and farther away from shore. We had to go now or we definitely would lose it. We stripped off our clothes and resolutely stepped into the tepid water. Carl carried the flashlight and illuminated the tent, far out from shore.

Most of this part of the coast has a rocky bottom, which means that we would have had to swim out to the tent, making recovery almost impossible. We had chosen camp near a beach with a firm, sandy bottom, mostly free of rocks and life, so the going was fairly easy. Phosphorescence from tiny marine animals illuminated the water around us as we disturbed it with our passage. We interpreted this as a favorable sign from the gods. In only a few minutes we reached the tent, and although the water was more than waist deep and progress was difficult, we managed to hold the tent up almost out of the water and tug it back to camp.

I make it sound easy, but hauling a waterlogged tent through chest-deep water requires a high degree of heroism. The injustice of it all was that my bedding was inside the tent and was thoroughly soaked with salt water, meaning I had to sleep outside on a wet mattress, easy prey for every greedy insect within miles. Wrapping oneself with a sheet soggy from salt water on a July desert night defines what it is to be clammy.

When I told Fernando the next morning what had happened he laughed and apologized for not having warned me earlier.

"Aye Daveed, you should have asked me."

"What should I have asked you?"

"If it was safe to leave your tent there at your camp."

"And what would you have said," I queried, uneasily suspicious.

"I would have told you that a storm would take away your tent if you left it there on the beach." He looked at me with a wicked gleam in his eye and a mischievous smile of fake innocence.

Fernando was called a *brujo*, a shaman, by some of the Seris. He was known to disappear for days at a time with no other explanation than that he was in the monte or bush, although on one occasion he was really hiding from the police.

While he definitely was not religious in the ordinary sense of the term, he would make frequent references to Christian mythology, generally substantially modifying the traditional talk and mingling Christian symbols with his own lore. He didn't speak of visions, but he could relate and interpret Seri myths, making them so convincing they almost lost their mythical character. Fernando would tell you that he knew spirits. From time to time he would carve from the white, soft wood of the elephant tree, a *santo*, a talisman similar to many Christian relics.

One day we were sitting in front of his shack watching the Gulf. Most Seris feel a frequent obligation to check the Gulf to make sure things are in order. We watched, fascinated, as a school of dolphins did their acrobatics far out to sea. I asked him to tell me why dolphins like to play so much.

Fernando explained that dolphins hadn't always lived in the sea. Long ago, even before the Seris inhabited the land, the dolphins were people with a language even better than human languages. They loved to frolic and spent entire days playing with a rubber ball on the beach. Their games took them farther and farther into the ocean as they would kick and catch the ball. Then one day they found it was more fun swimming than running, and one or two stayed in the water. Gradually the other dolphins joined them and that is how they are today, playing and frolicking and talking all the time, hoping that people will come out and join them in their games. The dolphins love people, he stressed, and will try to help them in emergencies. Of all the animals they carve I have always felt the Seris capture the spirit of the dolphin best.

The story as he related it must be widely known because Seris do not kill dolphins under any circumstances. They will sometimes kill sea lions, which also abound in certain parts of the Gulf, but only if they find a solitary animal, which generally indicates the animal is doomed anyway. I know of no case where they have killed a dolphin.

Fernando had a charm which accentuated his deeply spiritual qualities. For years he wore his jet-black hair long, cutting it only when the pressure became too great on most Seri men to adopt the appearance of the men of the dominant Mexican culture. He had an impassive face, as do many Seris, with lively eyes (when he was sober) and a smile that easily erased the serious and often dangerous moods which would change his demeanor.

He was also an ironwood carver of consummate skill, specializing in small sea turtles which he produced with remarkable accuracy. I have been involved in deep conversation with him while he was carving with a machete (the preferred tool for making ironwood sculptures). So accurate was he that he did not even need to look at the wood he was carving. The machete

Fernando Romero

would chip away at the wood ceaselessly, even if he was not watching. I must confess that it was a tad unnerving to have him look me in the eye while he talked and carved, yet his hands were amazingly unscarred. He would often walk through the village chipping away on a small carving as he walked.

Fernando, however, was horrible when he was drunk. He beat his wife Angelita mercilessly, and others report he once attacked her with a machete, trying to cut off her hand. He was known to have injured his children when he would attack them in a drunken rage.

One day while I was in Desemboque he appeared on the main street swaggering and boasting in both Spanish and Seri. He insulted another Seri, one who always wears a gun. Before long the street looked like a replica of *High Noon* with Fernando and Roberto Herrera, the insulted, facing each other. The insults appeared to me to be harmless enough, the worst I could understand being "You don't speak good Spanish," but apparently they were interpreted as invectives and grounds for assault.

Since Fernando was unarmed I was scared to death that he would be shot. I started for him, intending to pull him away and lead him home. Before I could reach him a hand grabbed me by the arm and stopped me. It was Campuzano, Capitán's father.

"Daveed, don't get in the middle of this. He is very dangerous."

I took Campuzano's words seriously. It was widely reported that he himself had been involved in a fight years previously with a brother of Fernando's wife and a death resulted. The details vary from account to account, but the incident looms heavy in Seri history. I also have an abiding respect for Campuzano's analysis of events and people. He does not issue idle warnings.

I stopped in my tracks. Fernando, however, had seen me coming and had also been able to read my intentions. He turned on me, forgetting Roberto, whose hand was still held dangerously close to his .45 pistol.

"And you, stupid gringo, what do you ever do for me, tu pinche gringo?"

I made no attempt to reply to the insult, but pleaded with him to go home. Luckily for both of us he turned and staggered toward his house, still swearing at me and stopping every few steps to shake his fist. Drunks are usually laughed at by the Seris. In this case no one smiled. For a long while the crowd lingered by the store, speaking softly but sometimes heatedly in Seri. Roberto Herrera sauntered nonchalantly back to his house. Once again I felt like an ineffective outsider, even a meddler, but maybe, just maybe, I had saved his life.

The next morning Fernando came up to my ramada carrying a paper sack, which he handed me.

"This is something good for you and your family. You'll really like it."

The bag was full of fresh shrimp and three lobster tails. I thanked him, but he only nodded, gave a brief, half smile and left. He must have had one terrible hangover. That night we feasted. Even my son Chris, who doesn't like shrimp, had to admit they were delicious.

Two days later I stopped by Fernando's house to chew the fat. Although Seris do have outbursts of temper from time to time, for the most part they quickly forget and do not appear to harbor grudges. Fernando was carving industriously on his specialty, sea turtles. These exquisite little figures, no more than three inches across, captured both the character and the motion of the turtles, the caguamas.

On the ground next to him was a ceramic bowl. Inside it were a package of blue and red dyes and a translucent piece of rock.

"What are those, Fernando?" I asked him.

"It's paint for face painting."

"Who paints faces around here?"

"Angelita, my wife. You should let her paint yours."

"Would she do it for Patsy and Chris?"

"Of course. Just ask her."

Face painting is an art that at the time was in danger of disappearing and I was delighted to have a chance to do a little cultural preservation. Angelita came and stood in the doorway when she heard her name mentioned. As is the case with most Seri women, she refuses to speak or does not know how to speak Spanish, although she understands it well.

"Aahssah," she replied. Yes, she would love to paint our faces. Her smile revealed her eagerness to demonstrate her prowess.

Face painting used to be a regular feature of Seri life. Normally, only the upper half of the face is used and the designs painted are very precise. Each woman had her own unique, intricate design telling a different story. Men, too, used to have painting done, but only on more special occasions. Designs for men were generally little more than a few lines, although the resulting pattern could be complex. Even young children would have their faces painted when the occasion merited it.

Nowadays, the only time painting is done is when a Seri girl wants to flatter a young man, when a puberty festival takes place, when someone (usually an outsider) pays for it, or when some special occasion requires it, as when a Seri fisherman captures a leatherback sea turtle. These turtles are so rare that this happens only once every few years.

When the turtle is captured, it is brought in alive and a great four-day celebration begins. The huge animal, frequently weighing more than 500 pounds, is kept in a specially-designed shelter and all manner of dances are performed around it. The creature is fed, its carapace painted with bright designs and it is given water. After four days it is released, apparently none the worse for wear. This latter is just as well, for the leatherback sea turtle is an endangered species, quite rare even in the best of times.

Now Angelita would be painting the faces of some gringos and she would have an opportunity to practice and demonstrate her artistic ability. I went back to the ramada and asked Patsy and Chris if they wanted to be painted. Both did, although Chris was rather tired, still recovering from the sting of a stingray only the day before. Word spread quickly through the village and as we trudged down the beach we were joined by a crowd of urchins, a few young girls eager to see the exhibition and several nondescript dogs.

For the next two hours we sat very still as Angelita applied the paint with quick, firm strokes. Her principal brush consisted of a couple of horsehairs that gave a strong stroke yet permitted the painting of considerable details. Fernando watched from a distance, not wanting to appear overly interested, but looking quite satisfied, I thought.

In the past, the colors used by the face painters were natural, the blue derived from rocks, the red from plants and the white from a soft stone. Now only the white is made from natural sources, it is much easier to purchase small packets of powdered tempera dyes which seem to do as well as the natural ones, but aren't nearly so pretty.

Angelita's finished products were marvelous intricate mazes of red, blue and white. Tiny dots, surrounded by varying rings and lines, covered about one-third of our faces. All the designs were different, for, as Angelita explained, each was appropriate to the individual.

The onlooking crowd seemed to take the operation quite seriously, for the usual levity was more or less absent. Fernando looked around for approval from time to time and must have gotten it, for we frequently heard the peculiar cooing sound that Seris make when they approve of something. Face painting is still a serious business.

When Angelita was done she stood up, indicating the job was finished. Fernando nodded his approval and the crowd looked pleased, if perplexed at the gringos' whimsical desire for face painting. For the next few hours we proudly wore our face painting, generally to nods of approval. Then the heat of the day made us sweat and the paint began to wear off.

On the next trip I brought Angelita a bolt of fine, blue cloth. She was pleased with it and knew that her work had been appreciated. As is the case with all Seris nothing is ever done for free. Every favor must be returned, generally with a material good. For gringos the standard doesn't quite hold up, for favors bestowed upon Seris by gringos do not require reciprocity.

After that time Fernando always seemed friendly to me and even visited me in Tucson not long before his death. Even when he had been drinking he remained urbane. I just wish that his urbanity had extended to his family as well. He was an exemplification of how destructive alcohol can be.

Fernando died early in 1986. His death was an incalculable loss for the Seris. He was an irreplaceable repository of knowledge and a potent spiritual force. No one, I fear, exists today to take his place, either as a brujo or as a man deeply versed in Seri lore. And no one will ever make such a lovely ironwood turtle.

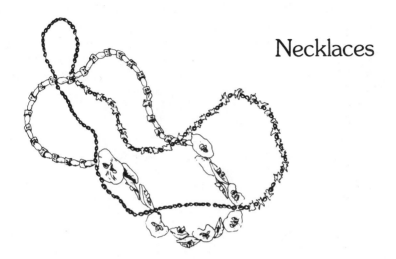

Necklaces

Tourists usually arrive in Desemboque exhausted by the long, bumpy, dusty ride. Although the road to Puerto Libertad is paved, the remaining dirt stretch of fifteen miles is still a rough trip and people head for Oscar's store for a soda pop before doing anything else. Frequently that is impossible, for within a minute of the tourists' arrival everyone in town knows it and the women gather their bundles and head for the tourists' car. The result is that the first thing the visitors encounter is a group of women offering necklaces and carvings for sale. "Offering" is probably too mild a term, for the tourist is likely to be besieged by women who inundate the prospective customer with necklaces.

By the time the outsider finds Oscar's, they generally find access to the storefront cut off. I have watched many gringos try to make their way to the store and then give up; too polite to simply push their way to the counter, they gradually become engrossed in the wares being offered.

Much has been written about Seri ironwood carvings; little attention has been paid to necklaces. This is unfortunate, for necklaces, which both men and women have worn for as far back as any Seri can recall, reveal far more about the Seris than do their carvings. Carvings were developed mostly as salable art objects in response to tourist demand. Necklaces were originally made by and for Seris. Ancient photographs depict men wearing elaborate necklaces similar to those made today.

Sometime in the 1950s, although they were wearing necklaces less themselves, the Seris found them to be a highly marketable item. Since that time they have proved a stable source of income and have been a source of immense creativity among the makers, almost entirely women. Their designs include imaginative variations on the single necklace, decorating a plain strand with rosettes of gaily colored shells and bones and creating items of personal decoration that have justly become popular items in gift shops throughout the southwestern U.S. (I am told that late in 1985 U.S. customs began cracking down on imports of the necklaces, invoking some provision of customs law that requires an export permit for wildlife or parts of wildlife. The importer must now list all species involved, a discouraging prospect for the importer of Seri necklaces.)

Most outsiders who visit the Seris buy several. There are so many and such a variety that it is hard not to. Outsiders long ago recognized the necklaces' appeal. At one time during the 1970s, Mexican fishermen swarmed into the villages buying on the spot all available necklaces without regard for quality. Taken to San Felipe on the Baja California coast the necklaces were sold at highly inflated prices to tourists who flock there from Southern California. The quality of necklaces quickly deteriorated and there must have been a sharp decline in snail and shellfish populations in the Desemboque area. I don't know what happened to put a stop to the practice, but mercifully the binge didn't last long.

Since the Seris originally made them as personal adornment, the necklaces reveal much of Seri material culture. One of the first I saw was made of hundreds of tiny yellow-orange flowers strung on thread. The blossoms were the dried flower of the Flor de San Juanico *(Jacquinia pungens)* which has the unique property that when soaked it swells and opens to almost its original size. As it dries it gradually shrinks once again to the dried dimensions. It appears this adornment could retain its fresh loveliness in times of prolonged lack of rainfall when natural flowers were absent because of drought. When all the desert world appeared grey, brown and bleak, the shrivelled-up necklace could be tossed in water and in only a few moments flowers would appear.

When I first met the Seris, another popular design found alternating black seeds *(Viscainoa geniculata)* about an eighth of an inch long and snake vertebrae. The reptile bones were boiled to remove any remaining flesh, left in the sun to bleach, and then strung alternately with several of the seeds. The black and white made a startling contrast. Often a rattlesnake's rattle would dangle from the bottom of the necklace, once an important part of Seri adornment, now more a marketing strategy. As these items became popular, the rattlesnake population must have dwindled dramatically. Rattlesnakes' nocturnal habits must be a godsend to their preservation, for

Eva Lopez

any found during the day are summarily executed, skinned, eaten, and de-rattled. The bones are then boiled and strung into necklaces.

As popular as the snake necklaces became, those made from all but the tiniest snakes were a hazard for the wearer, for the vertebrae are sharp and the weight of the necklace would pull the sharp points of the vertebrae into the wearer's neck, making the item rather uncomfortable to wear unless the neck was buffered with a couple of layers of clothing. When the Seris would wear them, usually for tourists' benefit, it would always be with a jacket or a blouse and scarf protecting the neck. Typically, however, the tourist would discover this only after returning home and wearing the necklace for the first time. At the suggestion of some regular gringo visitors the makers left vertebrae off the part of the necklace that touches the neck, but many makers ignored such a subtlety.

Most of the early commercially produced necklaces consisted of decorations strung on discarded monofilament fishing line, of which there is always an abundance on Desemboque beaches. Much of it was recycled from old nets that had become torn or tangled. This arrangement was economical, for new line was a costly item for the Seris, but it made for problems with the necklace. The old line, generally bleached by long exposure to the desert sun, would tend to twist and tangle, preventing the necklace from lying flat on the wearer. Few women were enamored of a necklace that would twist like a telephone cord when it dangled free. Often those of us who purchased some of the earlier products had to restring them on a new line or a finer thread. As the Indians became more affluent, however, they began using new fishing line and the problem diminished.

Another Seri favorite, rather uncommon now, was a shell necklace with five to ten postage stamp-size cloth bags of various colors strung onto the ornament. These bags often contained special herbs or other substances believed to have important powers. Sara Villalobos was especially inclined to make and sell this sort, extolling its virtues in protecting the health while at the same time trying to wheedle a few extra pesos for a cup of coffee. I am inclined to accept her promotional claims, for it appears to have worked well for her. I only wish that I had kept some of her masterpieces instead of having sold them. A trader's life is full of contradictions.

Most of the necklaces were composed of various sea shells ranging in size from tiny—no more than one-fourth inch in length—to large—as big as two inches long. The finest product was made of minute snail shells which had to be found by tracing the path of the snail in wet sand at low tide. It might take a woman two days to find all the snails for one necklace. The finished product was a delicate and colorful addition to anyone's wardrobe, showing the numerous shades of rose and purple associated with seashells.

After the snails were found, the shells would be cooked to remove the animal matter. Sometimes the cook would be in a hurry and particles of snail would remain in the shell. The resulting necklace would carry a definite reminder of the sea from whence it came. Traders sometimes had to sniff through hundreds of necklaces to find one that stunk of rotting sea food and befouled the whole lot. I once found one, buried among a few dozen, that must have been strung with live snails. The stench lingers in my mind to this day. Even with carefully cleaned shells, an odor remains. Every once in a while one can sniff the aroma of the sea in necklaces made years ago.

Producing necklaces requires the gathering of materials, mostly from the natural environment in which the Seris live, both the land and the sea. One of the more imaginative artists is Elvira Valenzuela, also an excellent basket-maker. From time to time Elvira would undertake the making of a sappim or huge basket which, upon its completion, is always greeted with an elaborate fiesta. I recall one which took more than a year for her to make. She interspersed her basket-weaving with the making of a lot of fine necklaces.

Elvira not only made many necklaces, she also produced a lot of food by gathering shellfish from the sea. As she was a widow and none of her daughters have husbands to assist in obtaining food, her family benefitted greatly. Lots of the shells wound up on necklaces.

One lovely morning I was chatting with Elvira and her daughters Angelita, Dolores, Manuela and Anna. Their complex, a prefabricated house and a couple of corrugated cardboard huts, is located on a knoll near the water's edge, surely one of the best lots in all of downtown Desemboque. At high tide one can throw stones into the water while sitting in the doorway of one of the huts. I coveted the site many years ago when it was still vacant and tried to obtain it for a house of my own. The reputed owner, however, declined my generous offer to lease it from him. "No, David, I can't let you buy it. Some days we like to take picnics up there." I never saw him or anyone else in the village picnic, and the site was only an eighth of a mile from his own hut, but he clearly didn't want me there. I don't know how Elvira and Angelita obtained the site.

On this particular morning the tide was going out rapidly. Abruptly Elvira rose, snatched up a bucket and headed for the sea, following the receding tide. I asked Angelita, quite a gatherer herself, where her mother was going. "For clams and shells," she said.

It seemed appropriate enough. In the Seri language, the name for Desemboque means "Place of the Clams." When tides are very low, large expanses of tidal flats are exposed. The women and children hurry out and dig for small butter clams and various shellfish until the sea rushes in again, claiming the clam beds.

I lost no time. Grabbing a bucket from my van, I hurried after Elvira, catching up with her just as she was squatting down to dig in the wet sand.

"May I dig here also?" I asked, knowing she could hardly refuse.

"Aahssah," she replied. She had nothing to fear from being alone with a man. She was quite old and "safe" and besides, there were many other folks around digging.

I dug frantically with a tablespoon, encountering numerous clam-size pebbles, but only a couple of clams and a few small snails. A half-hour later the tide began to flood the sand bar on which we were digging. I glanced into Elvira's pail. It was half full of clams and snails.

It wasn't fair I decided. I had worked just as hard as she and had about one-tenth the catch. I needed lessons I figured. When we returned to their hut, the daughters looked inquisitively into my bucket. They tried hard not to giggle I am sure, but couldn't control their laughter when I produced all of two clams.

Elvira used some of the clamshells for necklaces, throwing the remainder away after eating the clams. But she used all the small snails, boiling them, then sorting them by size in bowls where they would be dyed. She also picked up a dead shark on the sand and boiled the stinking thing until everything dropped away from the spine and the discs could be separated. Such is the natural history of many Seri necklaces.

In addition to sea shells and the shark vertebrae, which they incorporate in great numbers, the Seris use jojoba beans, glass or plastic beads purchased from Oscar, miscellaneous small ironwood figurines and clay beads, which they make and dye themselves. Occasionally they will use other plant parts and seeds, though seldom for necklaces made to be sold.

As traders began to demand necklaces of a certain quality, some women developed their art to a high degree. Patricia Moreno, a stunningly beautiful daughter of Eva, was especially precocious in this area. In her early teens she became proficient in producing large numbers of tiny ironwood carvings no more than an inch long. At the suggestion of a trader, she began to drill holes in the figures and string them, along with shells, on the necklaces. She then developed variations on this theme. Her completed necklaces would bring handsome prices.

Patricia's beauty, along with her vivaciousness and her happy-go-lucky mien belied her considerable talent. She viewed her artwork more with amusement than with artistic pride. In spite of her remarkable economic success, she continued to be most matter-of-fact about her products.

One day as I was chatting with Eva, Patricia, hardly seventeen at the time, showed me a piece of black coral from the bottom of Desemboque Bay which she had obtained from a friend. She showed me how, with a little buffing, the coral would shine like coal. I suggested to her that she incorporate the coral into a necklace. She responded joyfully to the suggestion and immediately went to work. With a hacksaw, she carved the coral branch into pieces about one-half inch in length. These she then drilled with a hand drill to produce a hole along the length of the piece. She then strung the pieces with some ironwood figurines and snake vertebrae into an astonishingly beautiful piece of jewelry. It took her and her sisters only a couple of hours to produce. I bought it from her on the spot, convinced that I had planted a seed that would establish a new industry. I had some misgivings about the project, since black coral is nowhere very abundant and removal of large quantities could cause ecological havoc on the floor of the Gulf. I also learned it is protected under Mexican law.

I needn't have bothered congratulating myself or worrying about the coral. So far as I know she never made another such necklace. She preferred to stick with the talent she knew she had, making large numbers of tiny, exquisite ironwood figurines.

The selling of necklaces also developed the marketing talents of some Seri women. Although women are typically quiet in the presence of strangers, they have a peculiar aggressiveness when it comes to selling items. As I noted earlier, some women would jab a prospective customer in the ribs in order to bring to the customer's attention that she wished to make a sale. In the case of necklaces, women become even more aggressive. They have developed an ability to carry a dozen or more necklaces, effectively using their arms as a display rack. With their arms extended they can also block all escape routes of the intended buyer, while exhibiting a baleful look of frightening proportions. At times they will urge a customer to partake of their wares by muttering, "Mucha hambre" (Very hungry), a sensible variation on their less subtle threats.

Particularly ominous are women with both a carving and necklaces to sell. They have learned that persistence generally works well with gringos. They will stick the carving in a tourist's face nudging him or her with it, then with the other arm extended, make sure that the poor soul cannot but run into a slew of necklaces. Sometimes a garment being worn by a tourist or an item the woman spies in the tourist's vehicle strikes the woman's fancy and she will indicate that she wishes to trade. The terms of the trade are seldom favorable to the tourist, but the Seris have become so aware of the weaknesses of tourists that the woman generally obtains what she wants. And for only a couple of necklaces. They seldom trade a carving or basket for anything that isn't new or quite valuable, but a necklace or two for a garment or an ice chest or Coleman stove always seems a good bargain. To them.

Mass production of necklaces has led to some pretty shoddy work. Cheap dyes are sometimes used to produce colors that appear glamorous on the beach, but which quickly fade after being purchased by a tourist. Ornaments on the older necklaces contained only natural colors or were dyed with hues laboriously produced from natural sources. These are seldom found now. Most of the dyeing, however, results in lovely colors which contrast brightly with the white of bones and the black of the Viscainoa seeds.

It was not unusual for women from whom I would buy carvings from time to time to present me with a gift necklace. One would simply hand me a necklace or two and say "Regalo" (Gift). After a while I became uneasy with these "gifts" for I learned the hard way that Seris always expect something in return. A gift meant that something was going to be expected of me. If I failed to purchase something the next time I saw the woman I was in for some heavy hostility and, I am certain, some pretty nasty gossip. In fact, I am now convinced that many of the stories circulated about traders, most of which are wildly inaccurate, stem from unrequited sellers who have bestowed such a gift necklace with the hope of selling more at a later time, only to discover that the gift which might incur an obligation among Seris had no such effect among gringos.

From the woman's standpoint the sale of necklaces must be a personally gratifying event. The carvings she sells are often made by others or are items that she only finishes. Baskets which tourists will buy require a degree of skill that not all women possess and a long investment of time. To make a necklace requires only a familiarity with the materials and a fertile imagination. The woman takes a piece of fishing line, often tying one end on her big toe, stretches the line out and begins to string. When buyers appear in town, she can turn several out in a short time and earn enough to buy food for a day or two.

From time to time a buyer can obtain necklaces made with small clay balls often dyed blue, alternated with another material. María Antonia Colosio, a grand old Seri and ethnobotanical consultant, first sold me an example of this kind of necklace in 1969 and sadly I have long since lost it. I believe she actually fired the clay so that the balls were hardened and resisted water. Some of the more modern ones will disintegrate alarmingly when they become moist so it is best to wear them in an arid climate and then only during the dry season. One also quickly finds out the extent to which dyes run. Many a lovely blouse has been stained permanently, much to the wearer's chagrin, by colors transferred from a necklace. I made it a practice quite early to wear or give as gifts only the sorts of necklaces I had seen Seris themselves wearing.

Every once in a while a Seri will make an object with only a commercial motive. One such item was a necklace I bought from a younger woman. It consisted of a couple of shells with a heavy ironwood cross, about two inches across, at the bottom. It was hardly a delicate piece, so heavy it would have been hazardous to wear while swimming. A friend had once asked me to buy any Seri cross I might find, so I dutifully purchased the piece. The cross wasn't so bad once it was removed from the necklace. In fact, it was a rather charming little item. I sent it to my friend in an envelope in the mail, not wanting to bother with wrapping it and mailing it parcel post.

About six weeks later he received it all right, but somewhat altered. The envelope had been utterly mangled by the cancelling machine so that in order to determine the address, the Postal Service had to piece the shreds like a jigsaw puzzle. The cross arrived without a scratch, but I suspect that the cancelling machine had to undergo substantial repairs. Once again nature triumphed over technology.

Ironwood, found only in the Sonoran desert, grows very slowly and someday sufficient ironwood for carving will be gone. As Mexicans clear more and more desert for other uses, and as the supply of dead wood is gathered for fuel and the carvings being mass-produced by non-Seris in Kino Bay, the supply is dwindling. In a couple of decades there will be no more.

The materials for making necklaces, however, will be replenished and continue to find their way onto Seri necklaces as long as there are Seris. The role of necklaces in preserving the Seris' knowledge of the desert and the sea will become more important, for they will still need to go to the desert and the sea to find the materials to string on their wares. In searching out the raw materials for necklaces, they will constantly replenish their knowledge of their environment. Our adornment and the cooperation of U.S. customs may be an important factor in the Seris' survival.

Chon (And His Friends)

Chon was a great friend of mine. Smart, reliable and handsome he was, and many were the hours we spent together. On my numerous visits I brought him gifts of food; he responded with affection and a hint of loyalty. Although he has long since died, he is an indelible part of my memories of Desemboque.

Chon was Luisa Astorga's dog. He was unique in that he was clean (an anomaly in Desemboque and most of Mexico) and also in that, while a fierce fighter, he was one of the few dogs in town who was friendly with my large, black Afghan hound, Mephistopheles.

Meph struck terror into the hearts of most of the Seris. While he never showed much interest in people, he had no tolerance for the onslaughts of Seri dogs, whom he routinely demolished in fights, even when there were three or four against him. His presence was a sore point with the local canines, who resented not only his arrogance and indifference to their noisy protestations, but also his haughty bearing, and perhaps even his pedigree. He would prance through the village, invoking storms of rage at each hut.

Meph's way of fighting was unknown to the roughhouse crew in Desemboque. He would knock his opponents down with his long paws and subdue them with a quick slash of his elongated, narrow head. Rivals seeking to grab his neck or head were usually frustrated because of his long hair and tiny head, which made a poor target. After a few such incidents, the Seri dogs would bark furiously at him, but would not approach within thirty feet or so.

Except for Chon. He not only showed no fear at all, but treated Meph like a long-lost brother, prancing up to him and nipping at his nose like a puppy. Unaccustomed to making friends with any dog, Meph was so disoriented by this behavior that he wound up tolerating Chon's presence.

Meph's reputation as a terror achieved for me my Seri name *Aajsh Copol Akaeet,* "Father of the Black Dog." Someone started the rumor, still circulating, that he was half dog, half bear. The Seris noted well how fierce Meph was in battle and inferred that his ferocity extended to people as well. When Meph would come dancing down the street, as Afghans are wont to do, all people around, except for a few stalwart men, would flee in fear. Chon would be following closely behind Meph.

Chon's acceptance of Meph showed how unusual he was, but there was more. Chon was an outstanding *chivero*—goatherder—and a protector of the Astorga household. He was also a sweet and gentle beast, a handsome animal with a nice golden coat accented by a white collar and paws.

Perhaps it was because of Luisa's care and frequent grooming that he was so special. He seldom left Luisa's side and always accompanied her and the other women of the family on their trips to the monte. Chon seemed to look forward to these regular hikes into the brush and viewed them as his recreation and his chance to protect Luisa. (Somehow the Seris have developed tough bladders and sphincters, for they seem to head for the bushes no more than a couple of times a day.)

Until recently there were no privies or toilets in Desemboque except for those constructed by the Mosers and the few Mexicans who lived there. The Seris merely continued as they have for countless generations, walking to the edge of town to the monte where there are plenty of bushes to relieve themselves. As the size of the town increased, this became a bit of a problem and when the Mexican government built permanent houses for the Seris in the mid-70s it was fortunate they also built toilets in the houses. The edges of town were beginning to smell pretty rank and, I suspect, were a health hazard, perhaps responsible for the high incidence of amoebiasis among the Seris. Unfortunately, the new toilets appear to work no better than any other toilets in Mexico.

At a dog show, Chon would not have attracted much attention. But he was a champion compared with most of the dogs of the village, mangy, cringing curs for the most part, who live a precarious existence, tormented by hunger, parasites, fleas and a multitude of skin disorders. On top of all this they must face the constant pranks of street urchins who consider dogs their rightful targets.

The Seris' treatment of animals is strange, at best, and only a few of their myriad canines merit mentioning because they are such a ragged, scurvy bunch. They are mostly a slinking crew, submissive and cowering, scavenging around the huts and along the beach for a bit of fish or other scraps to fill their chronically empty bellies.

In the spring, when the bitches come into heat, the town can turn into a rapacious, lascivious tableau, a sure education for the young and those of strong stomachs. Packs of drooling, panting, lustful males surround the unfortunate females, each hoping for a few moments of ecstasy and ready and willing to destroy any rival. Some battles that break out are fearful, bloody wars in which a lot of sexual energy is directed into a violent mayhem of canine bestiality. Few dogs escape unscathed and most bitches, when they finally bear their litters, produce an astonishing array of puppies of obviously varied paternity. So blinded by lust are many of the males, however, that they expend their seed on inappropriate targets, oblivious to the fact that what they have mounted is the inappropriate end of a bitch. I recall occasions when walking with my children that I spotted dogs mating and hastily tried to divert the attention of my innocent offspring to alternate features of the environment, but with little success, so spectacular was the riotous activity around the bitch.

As miserable as the existence of most Seri dogs is, it is made worse by the numerous kicks, pokes and stonings they inevitably experience. Seri children become expert at hurling stones at an early age and their accuracy can be uncanny, as every dog in the village knows. Frequently one hears some obnoxious cur barking relentlessly at night, followed by a yelp and a series of pained howls, then silence. Once again a rock, bottle, shoe or pan has found its target.

I describe the Seris' treatment of their dogs as strange, for as brutal as life appears for the beasts, the Seris are quite possessive of their dogs and truly seem to love them, permitting them in their huts and even allowing some of them (but only some) to sleep on their beds, tolerating almost all "doggy" behavior except the theft of food and the unforgiveable sin of being in someone's way. An experience of Jim Hills' illustrates the Seris' strange attitude toward their dogs.

One early summer day a dog fell asleep in front of the wheels of a car parked in front of Oscar Topete's store. When the driver started the vehicle, it took off immediately, running over the rear end of the poor mutt. Jim saw it happen and heard the squeals of pain from the dog. It was an ugly critter, much of its fur already gone, festering sores all over its body. Now it was mortally injured and in savage pain.

No one made any attempt to help the dog. Few even appeared to take any notice, so it lay, whimpering and gasping in the hot sun, apparently abandoned to its death. After a while Jim could stand it no longer. He picked up a large hammer from his truck, intending to dispatch the doomed animal with a sharp blow to the head. But as he lifted the hammer, a chorus of angry protests came from several huts, which he interpreted as warning him not to do anything to the dog. Jim got the message and put his hammer back in the truck.

The dog perished a short while later and was left there in the street. The next day someone had removed it but no mention was ever made to Jim of the incident. He and I could only conclude that Seris have what seem to be unusual beliefs and feelings about their dogs, attitudes that are hard for us to comprehend.

Since that episode I have learned there is a rationale behind the apparently irrational behavior. Dogs, some Seris have told me, are not ordinary animals. They are vested with supernatural powers. If they are killed or mistreated, they will bring punishment down upon the perpetrators of the crime and even upon those who are associated with the perpetrator. Older Seris can cite instances to prove their contention that dogs can bring evil to evildoers. While the belief is not universally held and is not observed as much in younger people, the elders are convinced that those who harm or kill dogs will be visited with evil in the future.

This leads them to allow dogs to survive after grisly accidents where we gringos would surely want to put them out of their misery. A dog that lives in Punta Chueca is a good example. This cur, while still quite young, was also asleep under the wheels of a truck. The vehicle started up and ran over his hind quarters, pretty well flattening them. In spite of the horrible wounds, however, the Indians allowed him to live, and survive he did, albeit with totally paralyzed hindquarters.

The marvel of this dog, however, is that he can walk. Note that I say walk, not drag. He has somehow learned to walk on his two front legs, balancing his paralyzed rear end in the air as he moves, a scene from Orwell's *Animal Farm*. Graceful he is not, but he is mobile.

Occasionally one sees superior-looking creatures such as Angelita Torres' dog Ekkim, Santiago Astorga's pet Juanito, and some of the bizarre creatures of which Amalia and Adolfo are fond, the Mexican hairless. These are an unforgivably ugly breed and could not possibly survive without human or divine intervention. They resemble a canine version of a miniature hippopotamus, but it must be said they are quite intelligent and affectionate.

Three or four of these genetic freaks are usually to be found in Adolfo's yard, one of whom will be in reasonably good health and the favorite of the family. One I recall was named "No Se Vende" (Not for Sale). For this select brute, Amalia each year fashioned a jacket to give some protection from the winter cold which normally leaves a hairless shivering and miserable. The hairless do have one clear advantage, they are free of the fleas that are such a scourge to other dogs. They are also relatively clean, a fact which works in their favor, for Adolfo and Amalia permit these special beasts to sleep on their bed, ruthlessly kicking out (literally) all other dogs. For most other Seris, a canine found sleeping on a bed lies in danger of severe pummeling.

And then there was Santiago Astorga's dog Juanito. He must have had some black Labrador in him, for he had a decent coat and was a good hunter. I liked Juanito because he never cowered but maintained his dignity, even if it meant having to leave the Astorga's yard from time to time to avoid the fearful attacks made on him by stone-throwing children.

One night Juanito began barking furiously in the desert behind the Astorga's house, one of the few permanent Seri dwellings at the time. Since most dogs routinely bark at night, no one paid much attention, but he persisted, his barks becoming more and more vociferous. Suddenly there was a yelp, a whine, and then continued barking, but with an added degree of desperation.

Santiago grabbed a lantern and went outside the yard. Juanito was following a sidewinder rattlesnake that was headed for the house. He had apparently blocked its way, and in the process had been bitten by the viper. Santiago killed the snake and brought Juanito into the yard.

Sidewinders are especially dangerous because they tend not to rattle; whether rattlers vibrate their tail as a warning or as a protection, no one knows, but the sound saves a lot of lives. Sidewinders also have a sideways motion, which is great for them, enabling them to move rapidly over the sand, but confusing for the opposition. In humans the bite of a sidewinder is seldom fatal (95% of human rattlesnakebite victims recover) but in dogs it can produce death in a few minutes.

When I dropped by the house in the morning, Luisa was trying to nurse Juanito through the crisis. His hip was swollen to ghastly proportions and his breathing was labored. The snake had already been boiled so that the backbone could be used for making necklaces, making positive identification difficult, but from Santiago's description (and my confidence in Seri taxonomic abilities) I knew it was a sidewinder and Juanito could die at any time.

Luisa stayed with the dog, comforting him and soaking the wound with an herbal potion she had brewed. When at noon he was still alive, I knew he would make it. The next day Juanito was walking around, a bit gingerly, but walking nevertheless. Two weeks later he was back to normal. It was not the first time, Santiago told me, that Juanito had been willing to sacrifice his own life to protect his family. Small wonder he was treated with respect.

Older Seris become very attached to their dogs as they find themselves of lesser importance to their families. Old people frequently are forced to wander around begging for food. Often they are accompanied by a young boy and a dog, especially if they are blind. The dogs provide both companionship and a degree of protection, for some street urchins seem to enjoy teasing old, helpless souls even more than they enjoy teasing dogs. A canine protector can be an effective deterrent to this kind of torment. The beasts must be patient, however, for the master or mistress can rarely afford to share any food with them. The old Seris have such difficulty fending for themselves that they cannot possibly provide food for their companion as well.

Most Seri dogs seem to be suspicious of gringos. Perhaps the Seris tell their dogs the same thing they tell their children: if they don't behave, an ugly gringo monster will get them. Since the message strikes terror into the hearts of children, maybe it does the same with dogs. But now and then you will run across a dog who is particularly fond of gringos. Chon was one of these and Ekkim was another.

Ekkim, a friendly mutt, was Angelita Torres' dog. Angelita was born about 1940 and is the matriarch of her family. She had a child many years ago but the father didn't want to be tied down and abandoned them. None of her three younger sisters, all of whom live with her, has married, although one of them also has a child. Angelita also helped care for her younger brother, who was crippled by polio as a child. Today he is an excellent carver, and the entire family produces first-rate sculpture and baskets.

Ekkim was extremely loyal to Angelita and she treated him well up to the day he died of cancer. Virtually every Seri dog is familiar with the ominous sound, "ist, ist," hissed at it when someone wants it out of the way, but I never heard that warning directed toward Ekkim. A small dog, an apparent mixture of Welsh corgi and German shepherd, he would bound around wherever Angelita went, much to her delight. He also had a peculiar habit of digging a hole every night when he slept outside. More frequently though, he would sleep, along with several other dogs and five or six people, on the three double beds that, situated side by side, filled Angelita's hut, leaving almost no room for anything else.

Ekkim took to Jim Hills and me, maybe because we fed him or maybe out of some perverse affection. He knew when we arrived in town. When we reached camp, about a quarter mile south of Angelita's hut, he would come running up, tail wagging, jumping up and licking us.

One night I thought I would see if I could sneak in to my regular campground. It had been a grueling drive down from Tucson, the road in horrible condition. I didn't reach Desemboque until 11pm, long after most Seris are asleep. I drove as quietly as I could through town and turned out my headlights a hundred yards before arriving at camp. I opened the door of my Volkswagen bus as quietly as possible and was just beginning to remove my camping equipment when I heard behind me a flapping sound. It was Ekkim's tail banging against the steel table I had leaned against the bus. No fooling that dog. I gave in and fed him.

That night Ekkim was superprotective. No coyote dared approach my tent, and a couple of other mongrels, who thought they might sniff around in search of tidbits, were driven off with a vengeance. As always, Ekkim dug his small hole near the door of my tent and slept there. Whenever I woke up he would stir, look up at me and then settle back down.

In the morning he was off, back to Angelita's hut. As he left, he gave me a look that said, "Daveed, if you need anything, just call."

Coyotes, although genetically similar to dogs, are considered by the Seris to be empowered by some alien force. They are believed to possess even greater power than dogs and are viewed as quite unique by the Seris. One older Seri woman relates that she heard one howl at 4 o'clock in the morning. She understood the coyote to be warning that on that day one of her sons would receive a serious wound with a lot of blood. Sure enough, later that day her son was playing with a pistol which accidentally discharged, wounding him in the shoulder.

Furthermore, coyotes will wreak a horrible revenge if you interfere with them. For this reason, one Seri reports that coyotes are not killed, but are respected as beasts of power and vision. Knowing the ways of coyotes and their incredible ability to survive man's most desperate attempts at eradication, I am inclined to agree.

Trader Scott Ryerson pointed out to me that the Seris' respect for canines is reflected in the fact that they seldom produce carvings depicting dogs. I have seen a couple, both by Aurora Astorga, which are superb pieces. Apparently the power of dogs is sufficiently great that carvers avoid even graven images of the beasts.

If the Seri culture is fortunate enough to survive intact for another thousand years, we may find that evolution has produced a superior breed of dog, one that thrives in the desert. For now, no matter how ugly, how miserable they may appear, the Seri dogs form an integral part of the Seri culture. Without them both the Seris and we would be poorer.

Sara

Old age can be hell in many places, but among the Seris it is worse. Both summer and winter climates can be miserable and the old people are often left to fend for themselves. The lot of the elderly among the Seris has improved, but not greatly, now that the Seris are no longer nomadic and only peripherally hunters and gatherers. The older and less productive people become, the more they are viewed as nuisances by the younger generation, and food, shelter, clothing and medicine are not generously provided. Frequently one of the younger children is assigned to the care of an elder, an indication of the relative unimportance of the task.

The reasons for this are not difficult to understand. As is the case with Eskimos, another group of hunters and gatherers, unproductive people place a heavy burden on the culture. Since most of Seri life is dedicated to providing food and shelter, individuals who cannot assist in the effort are a liability. Among the Eskimos, younger people used to set old people adrift on ice floes where they would soon perish.

The difference, though, is that the Eskimos believed that by sending their old people off they were ensuring their access to a better life beyond. That is, they were actually doing them a favor. I have not noted any such belief among the Seris, although there are frequent expressions of compassion for their problems by younger people.

The old people are a burden on the family and the rest of society, and so, for many, life is, as Hobbes put it, solitary, poor, nasty and brutish. For the Seri elderly, as for the elderly in our own society, old age is psychologically isolating and physically uncomfortable, fraught with physical ailments. The greater availability of medicine has alleviated some ailments, to be sure, but the mobility required of Seris in the past still seems to remain an attractive goal, even if the reality has vanished. Perhaps it takes a few generations of sedentary, affluent life to instill any sense of reverence for age. My culture has certainly not done a very commendable job of it. We have, in fact, created a new nomadism for our elders who now tend to be more mobile than their children.

Sanitation is still quite primitive in the villages and inflammations of the eye are not unusual, making blindness common among old timers. The constant desert sun, mixed with glare from the Gulf, and the dust and sand which frequently blow into the eyes, also place a heavy strain on vision. The Seris don't seem to view blindness as a tragedy. The inability of blind people to find their way works a terrible hardship on them and from time to time urchins will tease old blind people, deliberately leading them into obstacles. In spite of their often miserable lot, some blind people do rather well. One in particular is Alberto Villalobos, a blind ironwood carver, who gained fame not only because of his uncanny ability to carve without vision, but also because of the high quality of his art.

Care of the elderly, while improved somewhat in recent years is not what I would call "gracious." The ancient ones are reminded daily that they are a burden. Younger people, unable to put their parents in nursing homes as we do, are given to complaining to the elderly that they are tired of giving them food and clothing. Sometimes they give them nothing, forcing the old people to wander around the villages begging. They suffer from cold winds in the winter and often have no one to help them into the bushes to relieve themselves. Those fortunate enough to have assigned to them a child who acts as a guide to the bushes sometimes face torment from the very children supposed to assist them.

Few chairs were available in Desemboque until recently. After a few decades the elderly have spent thousands of hours sitting on the ground and getting up and down. At the risk of being unscientific, I suspect this is a reason for the nearly universal presence of arthritis in older people. For many, simple movements are painful. I often have had my legs go to sleep while sitting with the Seris and have experienced an unpleasant stiffness upon arising. But I can go home to my comfortable chair. They cannot.

Seldom are tears shed when an extremely old person dies, unless that person had special significance. Even upon the death of Chico Romero, a grand old warrior as close to a chief as the Seris ever had, not a great deal was done by the Seris to mark the occasion.

Chico, gracious, garrulous, gentle, picturesque and fascinating, suffered in his final years from blindness and the same privations that most old people come to know. Celebrated for his personal beauty and dignity among many non-Seris, he was, nevertheless, forced to beg like other old people and to be led about by a boy who frequently tired of his responsibility. Chico was taunted by younger people who often laughed at his difficulties. In spite of all, he remained cheerful and dignified to the end. Often he would peddle pathetic dolls and necklaces or broken carvings he had tried to repair. Even when he was unable to make a sale he remained jovial, always willing to sing one of the old songs or tell a tale of the old days. It became a well-known joke that Chico referred to me as "Barril" (Barrel) instead of "Daveed", apparently because he misunderstood my name when he first heard it. To this day some of the men who were teenagers when Chico was still alive refer to me as Barril.

While Chico Romero was not celebrated by the Seris during his life as we might have, his memory is strong, making me wonder why he had to suffer so while he was alive. More than ten years after his death I played to a group of Seris a tape recording of Chico singing some Seri songs. Almost all of them were instantly able to identify the singer as Chico. They recalled him with fondness.

One morning I was chatting with José Astorga when another incident occurred which will give some idea of the horror of old age among the Seris. I knew the Astorga family well, having spent countless hours with them, chatting, watching, asking questions without end. I slept many times in their house, ate at their fire (for a price) and helped them sell their carvings. This particular morning I noticed that Santiago and Chalió, two of José's sons, were building a large box.

"What are your sons up to, José?"

"They are making a casket."

"A casket! For whom, me?"

José stopped chipping away on the carving he was producing. "It is for my mother. She died last night." He stared off into the distance for a few seconds. Then he went back to his work.

I hadn't even realized his mother was alive. I guess they had kept her pretty well stashed away in the house.

Later that afternoon they buried her. Present at the burial (done in Protestant Christian style) were six people: the Mexican evangelical minister and his wife, two of José's sons, one of his daughters and I. The pastor said a few words, led the singing of "When the Roll is Called Up Yonder" in Spanish, and ended the ceremony. I helped cover and bury the casket. That was it. I have never heard her mentioned since, a phenomenon often found among Indians who consider it inappropriate to speak of the dead.

So old age is no bed of roses in Seri country. Sara Villalobos had it even worse than most. It is bad enough to face old age with relatives who will probably not treat you very well. It is even worse to face it when you have no close relatives. Most of Sara's family were drowned in a boating accident a couple of decades ago, so she had few relatives on whom she could rely for anything. She lived with a niece and some grandchildren and although they offered her some sustenance, she faced the terror of old age with even less security than the average Seri.

But Sara was also profoundly resourceful, an astute observer of humanity, and cagey. For her, the increased number of North American tourists was a godsend and she took every advantage of them, developing a demeanor so appealing that her modest requests for food could never be denied. In her later years she carried with her a coffee cup and a bundle of things wrapped up in a kerchief, items she would usually try to sell to tourists. She preferred North American coffee to Mexican (Seris and many Mexicans claim our coffee is stronger than theirs; many North Americans claim Mexican coffee is stronger than ours) and knowing that few gringos were without it meant she generally had access to a bountiful supply.

In addition, Sara managed to beg a lot of clothing, food and money, both for herself and for her adopted family, with whom she was happy to share. Her line was a simple, yet effective one: "Give me coffee and food. I'm old and sick and very hungry. Give me money to buy food."

A more effective beggar never existed. Her need was real and obvious. Few could resist her appeals. Sara always wore an ancient black blouse and skirt, colors of mourning in remembrance of her lost family, and her tattered appearance accentuated her poverty. But there was also a side of Sara that few North Americans had the chance to see. She had a raucous, racy sense of humor, marvelous in a person who had experienced the tragedy Sara had.

When I first came to know Sara she was probably in her early seventies although she claimed to be ninety. Seris keep no track of age, so although a few recqrds are available it was generally hard to date some of the old-timers. At that time she was selling poorly made carvings which she would collect from the few distant relatives she still had, turning over to them most of the money she would receive.

For hundreds of years Seris have made ceramic dolls, about four or five inches tall, quite similar to figurines produced by the ancient Minoan civilization and also similar to Hohokam ceramics. While the real historic significance of these is a subject of controversy, one explanation, apparently favored by contemporary Seris, is that they were playthings. They bear a resemblance to fertility figures found elsewhere, with exaggeratedly large breasts and sometimes even female genitals. Some Seris still make these, entirely for tourist trade I think, and Sara is one who made them a decade ago, aggressively marketing them to the occasional gringos who passed through Desemboque.

These ceramics were the basis for wonderful ironwood sculptures, often more than twelve inches tall. The best were graceful creations reminiscent of madonnas, feminine, but quite chaste without any sexual overtones except for the breasts. They have become popular with tourists and well they should, for many of them would enhance any museum. The worst of them, however, are clumsy contortions.

One day Sara was trying to sell me one of the madonnas. I was reluctant to buy it for it was poorly done, lacking in symmetry and, how can I say this, the breasts were small and uneven, lacking the normal polished finish. I stammered something about not needing any more of this particular kind of figure, hoping she would accept my feeble explanation. She did not.

"Ay, Daveed," she croaked, "You don't like it, do you?"

"No," I replied, "It needs more work."

"You mean it needs more of this," she giggled, grabbing her wrinkled breast through her blouse and thrusting it at me.

Sara Villalobos

"Well, yes, er, I mean, no, uh, well, you see . . ." I became inarticulate. Unfortunately there were several others around who began to laugh uproariously, enjoying my prudish embarrassment. Sara cackled with laughter and as she hobbled away, looked back at me with a wicked leer. She had won and she knew it. I didn't buy the figure, but I felt I had to buy some of the misshapen dolls and little crudely-made baskets that she always carried with her.

After that Sara knew she had me. She became a daily visitor to my camp, hobbling the mile and a half across the desert with her cane, her dog and a young relative. She steadfastly refused to believe that I did not drink coffee, but she was always successful in wheedling a few cents out of me so she could buy coffee of her own.

"Ay, Daveed," she would moan, "I am very old and sick and I don't even have enough money to buy coffee for my cup." And she would again show me her ancient enamelled cup.

I would look her in the eye and she would give me a look of fake suffering, concealing a giggle. "How much is a packet of coffee?" (Coffee is sold in individual packets in Mexico.)

"Fifty centavos. Give me two pesos."

"Good. That will be enough for tomorrow."

And she would take my money and sit around a while, scolding me for not having a woman around or for not bringing my family with me or for not bringing her clothes and blankets because, as anyone knows, she was terribly cold and had no blankets and suffered from many infirmities. The next day she would be back, needing more money and some of my food, complaining (quite justifiably) that my dog had better food than she.

Sara's humor was also bestowed on other Seris. One day she was sitting in José Astorga's yard trying to sell some of her little things. She always had with her a small basket of trinkets, beads, necklaces, herbs and dyes all wrapped in a kerchief. She had laid out on a cloth all the wares she was hawking, trying to sell them to Jim Hills and me. We were trying to be polite but firm with her, since we had serious business with José, namely trying to get him to pay back some of the money we had loaned him.

She apparently began to tease José in Seri, for other Seris began to laugh, not at us, as was usually the case, but at José. José tried to parry her barbs but didn't appear to be very successful. After several minutes of apparent taunting, José had had enough. He reached over, put his calloused hand down her blouse and tugged at her breast. The crowd roared with laughter, as did Sara. But she, not to be outdone, waited for her opening. After he resumed work on his carving she leaned over to him and grabbed his crotch, knocking him off balance and taking him completely by surprise. The crowd exploded into hysterical laughter. For a moment José lost his composure, desperately wanting to fight back. But there was nothing he could do and he knew it.

Sara was never a busybody, but she was scandalized by the shameless behavior of gringos. She once upbraided me for sleeping as late as 7am. I asked her why I should get up with the sun and she told me, "Only lazy people stay in bed." Dutifully corrected, I never again allowed the sun to be up for long without rising. (Not that I had much choice, for with the sun came music blaring from radios, the clink of machetes and hatchets on ironwood and the hum of outboard motors as fishermen departed.)

She chastized Patsy and me once when she saw that Suzannah did not sleep with us in our tent. We had adopted Suzannah when she was five months old. The Seris knew all about it before we completed the adoption procedures, a phenomenon they could not fathom since the birth of a child is a welcome event for them and extended families are always available to care for any infant. When Suzannah had been with us for a couple of weeks, we brought her down to Desemboque. The Seris made a great fuss over her, calling her *Sheekj Copool* (Little Black Thing) because I had explained to them that Suzannah's natural father was black. To this day the Seris still coo over her and are very fond of her, now a grown woman.

But at five months she was sleeping in a portable crib covered by a ramada and mosquito netting, right next to the tent in which Patsy, Chris and I slept. Sara gave me a severe scolding. Suzannah belonged in the tent with us she informed me, even though the tent was designed for only two people. Every baby should sleep with its parents.

Sara is dead now, no longer spoken of by many Seris. Until her last days she remained a familiar figure, hobbling about with her cane and her dog, wheedling this and begging that, somehow managing to survive the rigors, pains and sorrows that old age brings in an unsophisticated folk culture. Until the last, she continued to cultivate (or manipulate) the acquaintance of the increasing numbers of North Americans who visited Desemboque.

She brought into old age a good deal of humor and dignity, qualities which rarely appear in our culture, much less in one only a generation removed from primitive. And now, years after her death, some still speak fondly and lovingly of her, recalling her exploits. No one could receive a greater tribute from her people.

Living off the Desert and the Sea

"Daveed." A whisper.

"DaVEED!"

Two voices. I opened my eyes and looked around. Barely light. It couldn't be more than 5 o'clock in the morning. There must be some emergency.

"DAVEED!"

I unzipped the netting and slipped out of the tent, trying not to waken Patsy and Chris.

Standing near the tent were Carmelita Burgos and Lidia Ybarra, single women in their late twenties.

"¿Que es?" (What is it?) I tried to whisper.

Carmelita blurted out something in Seri.

"¿Como?" (What?) I asked.

She repeated it. I picked up something about a saguaro. The rest was unintelligible, except to a Seri.

Finally Lidia intervened.

"She wants you to take her to gather saguaro fruit. Why don't you?"

It was fortunate Lidia was around. As an unashamed "liberated" woman, Lidia felt free to speak Spanish as well as to pursue with unabashed aggression various liaisons with men. She was comfortable interceding with gringos on behalf of other more traditional Seri women who were less adept at Spanish or more reluctant to speak it.

Seri woman carrying a load of cholla and torote

They waited expectantly. They knew I was a soft touch.

It wouldn't be such a bad idea. I had heard stories of expeditions to gather saguaro fruit and I needed to get into the hills to obtain a good chunk of ironwood so Aurora Astorga could make a special sculpture for me.

"All right. When shall we go?"

"At eight o'clock."

That was fine. "Eight o'clock" meant nothing at all, since in spite of their newfangled watches, the Seris observe designated hours only with the roughest of approximations.

I tried to go back to sleep, but the sun was coming up and sleep would now be out of the question. Everyone else in the village was rising and within a matter of minutes the sounds of Mexican music projecting from transistor radios, along with the steady chop-chop-chop of ironwood being carved, would make sleep impossible. Instead, I went looking for a couple of men to go along and help cut the ironwood, a task I couldn't handle alone.

A couple of hours later I was driving north, the Land Rover packed with ten Seris of varying ages. Not represented were girls under ten years of age. According to some, a taboo precludes their involvement and they are not permitted to handle the saguaro fruit.

We left the sandy coastal plain and its forest of cardón cactus that dwarfs the saguaro. As we squeezed through the narrows of the Río San Ignacio, a huge river system that runs at most a couple of hours a year, the Land Rover almost became stuck in the sand. As the great machine churned over boulders and through deep sand, I thought I was giving the Seris a taste of a Marlboro Man. They were unimpressed, giggling and laughing at all the bumps, envying the affluent gringo trader who had enough money to own such a joy machine.

After an hour we reached a spot where I had earlier noticed a good ironwood tree with a huge dead branch. The women and children embarked to collect saguaro fruit and torote. The two men and I prepared to cut down the ironwood.

The limb I had located was about fifteen inches in diameter. One of the men examined it carefully, tapping it to assure that it was solid. To obtain the two large slabs I wanted (one would be given to the men who were helping me) we would have to make three cuts and avoid harming the living part of the tree. Each cut would take close to an hour because of the thickness of the wood and its iron-like (hence its name) density. Ironwood is so dense that it will not float. I swear it is as hard as iron.

I took one end of the two-man saw and one of them took the other and we began to make the cut. After ten minutes we stopped to sharpen the saw, a welcome rest. Cutting ironwood is the hardest work I know and we sharpened the saw more often than was actually necessary. Nowadays many of the Seris have chain saws but they fail quickly, the chains dulled and the bars burned by the extreme hardness of the wood.

About two hours later we were done. I was dusty, sweaty and dead tired. I had brought no food and my water was warm and stale. It was the middle of June in the hottest part of the Sonoran Desert, but the Seris seemed barely warmed up and in no hurry to return. The men observed my weakness and misery with little sympathy. I wanted to be back in the village buying carvings and necklaces with shade and cool drinks available. As I was cursing my lack of conditioning and improvidence at not having brought food, some of the women returned to the Rover, bringing with them several buckets of saguaro fruit. They offered us some of their harvest.

Saguaro fruit are delicious and satisfying. They taste like a fig soaked in cherry juice and the seeds are rich in oil. They fill you up like no other fruit I know. We ate them until our hands and mouths were stained red with the juice, carefully extracting the fruit with a knife from the fleshy, spiny jacket, not wanting to touch the tiny stickers which can make your hands miserable.

One of the men suggested that if we were to help the women we could go back sooner. Tired as I was, it was the best suggestion yet. So off we trod into the desert searching for fruited saguaros. We didn't have to go far. That year was a particularly good one for saguaro fruit harvesting. The women showed me how they lash together the ribs of dead saguaros to make a very long pole. They then raise the pole to knock the mature fruit from the crown of the cactus, which is often twenty or thirty feet above the ground. A boy stands below and catches the fruit in a cloth, trying to keep from being hit by the spiny coverings.

We collected the fruits for a couple of hours. Then it was indeed time to leave. After the interminable process of loading buckets of saguaro fruit, heaps of dead cholla branches, our batch of ironwood, some piles of firewood and the bundles of torote thrown onto the Rover's rack, we made our way back to Desemboque, a thirsty and dusty crew, but happy with our harvest of the desert's bounty.

I wanted nothing more than a nice shower and clean clothes, but I had to settle for a sponge bath and some cool water. In those days running water was almost non-existent in Desemboque.

On other occasions I have accompanied Seri women when they went to gather mesquite beans, the fruit of the cardón cactus and the fruit of the chain-fruit cholla. Mesquite beans are easy to gather and for centuries have been the basic carbohydrate of the Seri diet (as well as that of the Tohono O'odham of Arizona). They can be eaten fresh or cooked in many different ways, providing a nutritious staple, but one which is notorious for producing

Elvira Valenzuela picking cardón fruit

gas. The Seris tell me pinto beans are a good deal tastier, so the switch to pinto beans, while perhaps regrettable from a nutritional and ecological standpoint, is understandable.

Cardón fruit are easier to harvest than saguaro fruit, for they grow on the side of the arms, nearer to the ground. On one of my trips to Desemboque I came upon a group of Seris gathering the fruit of the giant cactus. They had walked up the San Ignacio riverbed for five or six miles and had accumulated huge bags full of the fruit, which is valued more for its seeds than its flavor. The seeds are a valuable source of oil and protein and store very well when heated and dried. Older Seris say that no Seri hut is without an *olla* or large pot full of these seeds, a valuable food source in lean times.

I have eaten the fruit and can't say much for its flavor except that maybe it might grow on you. The fruit is dry and not very tempting in appearance or texture. The seedy interior, with a fig-like texture, tastes rather like peanut butter, which may explain the Seri craving for the latter, which they devour by the quart when it is available.

The chain-fruit cholla is an important source of vitamin C and is believed by Seris to be good for stomach problems, colds and menstrual cramps. I once drew gales of laughter from a group of Indians when I picked up one that had been collected by them and started to take a bite out of it. Fortunately a young woman stopped me just in time, showing me that you need to cut off the outside first, because it, like most cactus fruit, is covered with tiny, but extremely sharp, spines. These stickers penetrate deeply, have a toxin on them that makes them itch and sting, and are almost invisible. The inside of the fruit is sour but pleasant-tasting, and is especially relished by children. It is still common to see a bucket of cholla fruit lying in the sun or to find piles of the skins scattered around huts from which they have been cast before the insides are eaten. In recent years Seri gourmets have learned that the flavor of the cholla is enhanced when a few drops of lime juice are added.

The desert is a bountiful source of food, but one of the most marvelous food-producing areas anywhere is where the desert meets the sea, for it is the sea, the Gulf of California, that provides the greatest harvest. It is an humbling experience to observe the Seri's encyclopedic knowledge of the Gulf and its marine life. They not only know all the fish, but are experts in the anatomy of various species. They can classify dozens of different shellfish. They have developed a means of harvesting edible seeds from eelgrass, a marine seaweed prolific in the Gulf, and the prime food for caguama.

The expertise of Seri fishermen is remarkable. One day Adolfo Burgos, Amalia's husband, let me join him and several others. After I had watched them catch a few large fish, expertly hooking them and then clubbing them on the head so they would not flop off the hook, I asked if I could try. Adolfo, always willing to let someone else do the work, was delighted. Just as I was taking the line, a shark struck the lure and I was almost pulled overboard. I was certain that it weighed several hundred pounds, but when, with some assistance, I was able to pull the beast near the boat, I saw that it was only a couple of feet long.

I wanted to show my prowess as a fisherman. One of the boys handed me the club and I pulled the shark out of the water, trying to rest its head against the edge of the boat so I could give it a solid whack with the club. Just as I swung, however, it jumped. I missed the shark completely and instead hit the fishing line that was taut on the edge of the boat—hit it so hard that I cut it in two, losing in the process the shark, who swam off angrily, and the expensive and hard-to-obtain lure that was dangling from its jaws. The Seris roared with laughter. Then, staggering by the rocking of the boat that I had caused, I dropped the club into the water.

Even now in times of hardship, the Seris will turn to their own environment for food. (Although not without a lot of grumbling. One of them complained bitterly to me that I was really stingy because I wouldn't buy the carvings he had for sale and consequently he didn't even have enough money for a soda pop.) Women and children still collect clams along the tidal flats and little boys still clamber over rocks picking off snails, sucking the poor creatures out of their shells on the spot.

Clams are not difficult to collect. To prove a point, I once spent the better part of a morning gathering a bunch. After washing them off, I proceeded to steam them and took them over to Campuzano's hut to show him and Aurora that I could survive even if I did have blonde hair. He joined me in the feast, even providing a lime for flavor, and smiled tolerantly when it turned out that half of the clams had only sand inside the shells. "That's why you are so skinny, Daveed," Campuzano chortled.

Hunting was an important means of obtaining food in the old days, less so today. The Seris love and crave fresh meat, a relative rarity even now. Formerly they had a more or less regular supply of caguama, whose flesh tastes rather like a rich roast beef. Now the turtles are almost gone, hunted to the verge of extinction, their eggs seized from their beach nests by gatherers eager to sell them to Mexicans who maintain the eggs eaten raw are an aphrodisiac.

The Seris used to hunt deer with bow and arrow, with limited success. More common was the snaring of rabbits. I once happened by the Moser's house while María Antonia, an older woman highly respected for her vast knowledge, was describing to Becky how she would prepare a rabbit snare and wear a stuffed rabbit head on top of her head while she waited near the trap. She developed a whistle that would attract a rabbit, but her talent was unique and not widely shared. Sometimes, she said, it would be hours before the rabbit would pass by and even then it would frequently escape. I suspect that a stone in the hand of a young person had a higher degree of success than a rabbit snare.

Today, hunting and gathering are becoming things of the past, as is evidenced by Oscar Topete's store. The tiny shack, no more than fifteen feet square, is crammed full of anything a Seri might want to buy. Customers lean on the counter and order their wares, which Oscar or a helper produces.

Oscar was born in the 1920s, one of the few Mexicans who has made his permanent home in a Seri village. For years he was an internationally-known singer and entertainer. He abruptly retired thirty years or so ago, and for reasons shrouded in obscurity, opened a store in Desemboque. Rumors are murmured among the Seris of parricide, prison escapes and amorous intrigues. Details are elusive.

Whatever his reputation, if you talk to Oscar for a while he will sooner or later invite you to the back of his tiny store, offer you a cup of café cappuccino and play records for you on his battery-operated phonograph of his appearances in the flashy nightclubs of the Southwest.

It is here the Seris purchase flour for their delicious fry bread, shortening, rice, macaroni, canned goods, potatoes, beans, and above all, sweets and soft drinks. From time to time Oscar brings in fresh meat, which the Indians snatch up in a hurry. In season he sells fresh vegetables and fruits. He brings fresh corn tortillas from Hermosillo (the Seris have never made tortillas, a strictly Mexican food) and will sell you a single Ritz cracker.

Lining the walls are various kinds of materials, blankets, jackets, blouses, toothbrushes, pots and pans, cosmetics, patent medicines, shampoo in individual-size packets, herbs, trinkets and diapers, batteries, and on and on, including, now, toilet paper and sanitary napkins. Every once in a while he will bring in a shipment of fireworks, which sell like, well, fireworks. Oscar will also sell you gasoline, dispensed with a large pre-measured pitcher from a 50-gallon drum, and occasionally kerosene and white gas for lanterns. His is a remarkable preservation of the old general store, still found throughout rural Mexico.

Oscar's store completes the transition of the Seris from a subsistence culture, reliant on personal resources for food, clothing, shelter and medicine, to a consumer culture, depending upon commodities produced by others for the satisfaction of daily needs. In no area is this transition more sweeping than in their food.

Today, except for Seri bread which some women still make, and occasional infusions of gathered desert foods, the Seri diet is indistinguishable from the Mexican diet except that it is perhaps inferior, since the traditional Mexican diet includes large amounts of fresh vegetables. The Seri diet is high in refined carbohydrates and fats and low in complex carbohydrates and, increasingly, protein, which is ironic, since fish and seafood once constituted the bulk of their diet. Now the major items are flour, shortening and sugar. Jim Hills once calculated that the average Seri consumes six large soda pops every day, a certain hint as to the cause of the terrible tooth decay and gum disease which so mars the Seris' appearance today.

Scenes of food gathering and displays of indigenous food in the Seri huts are gradually disappearing. The transition from natural, locally obtained food to imported diets signals the disappearance of Seri culture. Many of the older Seri women were superb cooks. Aurora Astorga once prepared for me some fish I had bought from another Seri. It was quite simply the best fish I had ever eaten. But many of the younger women have not had the experience of dealing with the native foods and have never learned to cook as their mothers do. They match our culture in the tragic loss of this ability.

Saddest is the gradual disappearance of Seri fry bread. Even though the bread is a nutritional nightmare, consisting almost entirely of refined flour and grease, it is a real treat. It is made by mixing flour, shortening, salt, water and baking powder into a fine dough, molding the dough into balls and then allowing them to rise, carefully protected from dust and animals. After the dough rises it is flattened into pancakes and deep-fried until brown.

It sounds easy, but don't be deceived. Seris are not normally preoccupied with the principles of high society etiquette, but they do try not to laugh too uproariously at outsiders. Their limits were tested, however, when Patsy (who is an excellent cook) decided to have a go at making fry bread. She followed the movements of one of the Seri women step by step, even waiting the same time to allow the balls of dough to rise.

The final result was disastrous, a soggy leaden mass saturated with grease. I offered one of the cakes to Campuzano. He tried to be polite but was able to chew only a small bite before turning white. He then passed it on to a child who made no effort to conceal his laughter and disdain. The child threw it in the dirt, then offered it to a dog who with fake dignity lifted his nose and walked away. Patsy was good-natured about it, but it was her one and only attempt. Brave soul that she was, the Indians didn't even humor her.

Flour tortillas and white bread have made deep inroads into their diet, along with greasy fried potatoes and lots of oily soups and stews made from canned ingredients. I am relieved that now Seris are not generous with their food, unlike the Mexicans of the culture that surrounds them. Only a couple of times in all my years with the Seris have I been invited to eat with them (on other occasions I have purchased meals). But it is just as well. Their current dietary intake makes me long for Big Macs and Hostess Twinkies. Once Jim and I were invited to eat in one of the huts—the fare consisted of potatoes swimming in grease, and white bread. I am sure the woman who prepared the food believed she was doing us a favor, serving us sophisticated North American cuisine.

I hope the Seris continue to eat enough seafood to keep their nutritional level above the point at which severe disorders erupt. In times when money is short, when North American buyers are not around to infuse large amounts of cash into the local economy, they tend to revert to the old diet. These periods of economic deprivation are probably nutritionally beneficial to the Seris. They must fall back on the food resources of the desert and sea around them. Once again the traders and merchants, while increasing the general affluence of the Seris, also undermine the integrity of their culture. Oh, well, I always rationalized, if they don't sell to me they will sell to someone else and I will encourage them to improve the quality of their work. I'm sure other traders used the same argument.

Even with the gradual decline of natural desert areas, sufficient resources are still available to maintain a large population of Seris in good health. I cherish the optimistic thought that maybe some day the younger people will rediscover the joy of gathering native foods and the wholesomeness of a diet rounded out by foods available in their own backyard. And some instinct, maybe from a collective unconscious, tells me there is no greater human experience than the sheer exuberance of a food-gathering expedition to collect one's own sustenance. Especially in the company of the likes of Carmelita and Lidia.

Eva

Evangelina Lopez wears a Seri face design permanently tattooed on her nose, not an uncommon practice for Seri women of middle age. I have never asked her how she came about that particular adornment, partially because she has had a rough lot in life and I didn't want to dredge up painful memories.

As a young woman, Eva was remarkably beautiful, with a warmth and sparkle and natural sensuousness that live on in her face today. She was quite the belle of the town of Desemboque. Then things began to go downhill. She fell in love with a Mexican fisherman, a jack-of-all-trades whom she followed to Tijuana, lured on by tales of the magic of the big city.

Seris seldom leave Seri villages except for brief trips into Hermosillo, 125 miles from Desemboque, or on fishing or gathering trips. During Holy Week it became a custom several decades ago for as many as possible to migrate to Kino Bay and make camp there. Occasionally individuals have journeyed to Mexico City, as a result of a government invitation and some have visited the United States to participate in Indian festivals, but only a few have left the villages on a permanent basis. Eva was one.

Whether it was because of economic necessity, a personal crisis or the only alternative available to her, Eva, finding herself abandoned in Tijuana, so the story goes, became involved in the low life of that border city. The sordid circumstances surrounding that difficult time left their indelible mark on her.

After some time she managed to find her way back to Desemboque. Jim Hills and I first met her there in 1968, selling carvings and demonstrating a most friendly demeanor. We spoke with her for some time because she was quite willing to answer in a most cheerful way our innumerable questions about the Seris and their lands.

By that time fate had been somewhat kinder to her. Whether by choice or by the fact that she was ostracized by her own people, Eva took up residence with a Mexican much older than she, Pancho Moreno. A diminutive man with a worn face, he was a good provider who had a decent head for business. He and Eva were good sources of information for outsiders who did not speak Seri. Eva, as the reader can guess, was not inhibited by the traditional reluctance or inability of Seri women to speak Spanish. They had several children, including two daughters of striking beauty, who became first-rate basket weavers and ironwood carvers.

Pancho was an entrepreneur. He would purchase carvings in a semi-finished state, polish them and sell them for a good profit. He raised an occasional pig, feeding it grain for good weight gain and sold the pork. The pork was of high quality and coveted by the Indians, whose supply of red meat is always uncertain. He would also loan money, although at high interest rates, which earned him the antipathy of those to whom he made loans. He had numerous other enterprises going simultaneously, all of which produced for him a reputation of being a tycoon, an exaggeration of course, for he was only relatively wealthy. He endured insults and the ostracism bestowed on his mate and their children, and remained friendly, knowing that the Indians needed him as much as he needed them.

Sometime in 1971, when things seemed to be going rather well for the clan, someone set fire to their hut. Some said the fire was set by an angry debtor, others said Pancho set it himself. Pancho tried desperately to save some of his belongings, burning himself badly in the attempt, he claimed. His heroic efforts were in vain. Their hut was completely destroyed, along with their tools and other possessions. Pancho later told me he had lost more than twenty thousand pesos ($1600) which had been buried in a box in the sand that constituted the floor of the hut.

Somehow Eva and Pancho recovered. They built a new hut, acquired new tools, clothing, and a stove and slowly re-established their niche in town. Pancho once again seemed destined to build an economic fiefdom

Eva and family

from his shack. Rumors began to circulate that he made money dealing in drugs.

The stories, inevitably embellished with utterly improbable claims, generally described Tepopa Point as a favored location for the running of contraband—dope, guns and appliances—the latter heavily taxed in Mexico. Frequent low flights over the area by what appeared to be Mexican police aircraft gave some credence to the rumors. Merchandise would be brought from the United States down the Gulf and exchanged there for marijuana and heroin. The appliances would go to Hermosillo, the dope to the U.S.

Although I never saw any proof of smuggling activity, it is certainly plausible. There are a couple of sites where a fairly large yacht could get close to the shore and make a delivery or a pickup. Because this section of the coast is irregular and isolated, the probability of getting caught was as low as anywhere on the Mexican coast. Or so the stories went. Furthermore, due south of Desemboque are a number of large playas or dry lakes that make excellent landing sites for aircraft. Some of them are a mile or so in diameter, perfectly flat and hard-surfaced, making a quick pickup or delivery easy.

And so the rumors spread. Pancho would frequently be gone for a few hours or even a couple of days with explanations on his part that seemed sort of lame. For example, he would claim he had to see a doctor or he had "business" to attend to. Whether or not he was telling the truth, few believed him and his reputation (and respect) grew proportionally.

One day in 1975 Pancho failed to return after telling Eva he would be gone for a while. She figured he had picked up a ride into Hermosillo. But the next day he also failed to show up. When he didn't appear after two days, Eva became upset. She had no way of making any official inquiries, so poor are communications in the area. Rumors again began to spread. This time the substance was that Pancho had been arrested for smuggling and would be in jail for a long time. Eva tried to get information from Hermosillo, but could find nothing. Another rumor placed Pancho in prison in Mexico City, while yet another had him killed in a shootout with the police.

At any rate, Pancho never returned. Evangelina, who had experienced tragedies before, took his disappearance in stride and managed to eke out a living by making necklaces and selling a few baskets and carvings made by her daughters. Fortunately they proved to be excellent wood carvers, developing a technique of stringing tiny carvings intermingled with shells into an exquisite necklace which became a bestseller. The clan was thus able to scrape together enough income to provide for their immediate needs. In time, another Mexican took Pancho's place, also named Pancho. This man was much younger than the previous Pancho, a shy, retiring individual who was a hard worker and good carver.

Then in 1977 the mystery partially unraveled. Word came into Desemboque that a whale had beached and died a few miles to the southwest, out toward Tepopa Point. For reasons as yet unknown, whales will sometimes beach themselves and resist all attempts at rescue. Pilot whales seem to be prone to this strange behavior much more than the common grey whales. When these huge-toothed beasts beach, it is truly a remarkable sight.

The report generated considerable excitement in the village. While fairly common in the Gulf, whales are seldom seen up close and their massive bones are treasured by Seris just as they are by North Americans. Several truckloads of Seris headed out toward the point, driving as far as they could, then walking the rest of the way to the place where the carcass lay, hoping to find large bones to use as decorations for their otherwise drab yards. Panchita, Pancho Moreno's eldest and most beautiful daughter, was one of those who jumped in a pickup to view the dead leviathan.

The group milled around the carcass for some time. Once they had seen enough of the whale, Panchita and her friends headed back across the desert in the direction of the pickup a mile or so away, choosing a different route to walk back, one they thought would be shorter. Seris love to explore the desert so they made their way in a leisurely fashion, stopping frequently to look at plants and throw stones at jackrabbits, playing games with each other in a picnic atmosphere. Each person chose a slightly different route, hoping to find some firewood or some treasure along the way that would serve as a momento of the walk to the whale.

About halfway back, one of the women gave a sharp call to the others; she had stumbled onto the remains of a human being, well scattered over an area of about half an acre. The rest came running up, including Panchita. They all commenced to scour the area. In the process Panchita discovered a skull and excitedly announced her discovery to her companions who were finding other bones and some personal effects of the deceased. The young women chattered with excitement, Panchita in particular being delighted with her discovery.

Then one young woman discovered a metal object half covered with dirt and stopped in her tracks. She carefully picked it up and found it to be a belt buckle. She called the others and they converged on her. One of the party immediately identified the buckle as being Pancho's.

His daughter was now holding the skull of her father. With a shriek she dropped the skull and hid her face in horror.

Various artifacts found verified the identity of the remains, but there was nothing to indicate how he had died. Others found an empty water bottle nearby and a young man found Pancho's wallet, its contents intact. There was no sign at all of foul play.

The story caused a sensation in Desemboque. Eva and Panchita received a remarkable amount of sympathy and for weeks speculation continued as to the cause of death.

And so the saga of the disappearance of Pancho Moreno was closed. To this day there is no clear explanation as to what happened. The most plausible story is that he suffered a stroke or heart attack while out on the desert, but why he was there remains a mystery. In all probability we will never know. Unexplained deaths are more commonplace and forensic pathologists scarcer in Mexico than in the U.S. Autopsies are not generally available except for the rich and important.

Today Eva remains in the same hut, a tall proud woman whose girth seems to increase with every year, as does the size of her clan. Two of her daughters have married Mexicans, but one has returned to live in the village and seems far more Seri than Yori (the Seri word for Mexican). Still rather apart from the social life of the rest of the village, Eva has perfected an act whereby she feigns anger to pressure tourists to purchase carvings and necklaces from her. I can attest to the effectiveness of her pitch and the guilt she can bestow on those who fail to purchase. She has discovered that sometimes tourists will buy items from her just to get her to leave them alone.

As Eva moves through her middle age, her face shows the hard times she has seen, yet she remains cheerful and hopeful, always waiting for the next tourist to purchase her arts.

When Eva becomes too old to work or produce she will have a difficult time surviving. Much of her clan, a bewildering mixture of Mexican and Seri, has been Mexicanized, and sad as it may seem, she may find herself forced to leave Seri country for the more hopeful affluence of Hermosillo. It will be a pity if she goes. My hope is the tragedies she has experienced will give her strength to endure the even greater pressures toward social change that daily bombard her people.

Yolanda Morales de Astorga

Love in the Seri Manner

It would be difficult to spend as much time as I did with the Seris and not become curious about their love lives. My curiousity was heightened both by their earthy language and by the beauty of the young Seri women who sometimes seem to be transformed overnight from innocent girls into seductive women.

The frankness with which the Seri people openly joke about sexual things has often reddened my cheeks. Older men in particular seem to relish the opportunity to make racy gestures, much to the delight of their audiences. Except for Sara, I cannot recall seeing women make obscene talk and gestures, for they are generally most puritanical, even prudish. But they join heartily in the raucous laughter that invariably accompanies these episodes.

There are many inconsistencies. On one occasion Adolfo took it upon himself to take me aside and inform me, with urgency, that a word I had just used in Spanish was a bad word. Yet on the same day I heard him use language that was not exactly pulpit material.

And while public displays of affection are almost unknown, no one seemed at all embarrassed when Lidia propositioned me in the presence of ten or so people. It was especially brazen of her, for Patsy and I were camped north of town with the children. I had walked into the village to do some bartering and to hang out with a couple of families. Lidia was there, enjoying the generally happy atmosphere that is so common in Seri households. I was seldom able to follow the conversation except when a Spanish word was thrown out, but was content to sit around and enjoy the good feeling I had watching the Seris living.

Lidia was, as usual, laughing and cutting up with the men, when she turned to me and said, out of the blue, "Daveed, wouldn't you like to sleep with me?" I muttered something stupid and inarticulate, wishing I could hide under a rock. The rest of the people looked at me, many of them grinning, obviously hoping for a new liaison to discuss. When I demurred, they seemed disappointed, but understanding. Lidia was widely viewed as a loose woman, but she was not particularly criticized and not ostracized as far as I could tell. It may have had something to do with her ability to speak passable Spanish and her willingness to sell other people's carvings for good prices. It may also have been her genuine concern for Seris, even those outside her own family, who were in need.

Pregnancies outside of marriage occur and not too infrequently. These can cause a momentary uproar, not so much because of the deed, but because of the question as to which person or which family is to be responsible to the mother of the child and her family. I have seen angry confrontations between two women, one the mother of a pregnant girl, the other the mother of the father of the child. The argument isn't complete without ritualistic shaking of fists and yelling that takes on a peculiarly musical tone. I am sure it is a deadly serious matter to the women involved, but to an outsider it appears to consist largely of bluffing, each side aware that the other must make certain moves. The consequences of the way the arguments are settled are of critical importance, of course.

There doesn't appear to be much stigma attached to a woman who has a child outside of a sanctioned marriage, but a proliferation of such events would undermine the structure of the family, the elaborate scheme of relations between families, and the way these relationships relate to a growing child's place in Seri society. It is not enough simply for a child to be loved (and Seri children are cherished). A child must also have a clear place in a family so that he or she will be able to determine their personal and cultural identities.

Frankly, I don't know how couples manage to make love without being seen. In every hut or house there are several people in each room (when there are rooms), as well as various guard dogs who, though whimpering, slinking curs during the daytime, become the image of a stern police dog at night.

One North American who has forever vanished from Desemboque was convinced by a Seri man that all he had to do to partake of the pleasures of a Seri woman was to pay her money and make arrangements to meet her in some wash near town. He decided to test this hypothesis, partly, I suppose, out of stern academic commitment to his anthropological discipline. "Somebody needs to document this phenomenon," he asserted. "Who is better versed in the rigors of scientific experimentation than I?"

He claims that he made payment, extracting a solemn promise that she would meet him at the appointed spot at a certain hour of the night. As he described it, he waited, with increasing carnal itching, and waited, and waited. She never showed up. Eventually he realized that he had been taken for several hundred pesos.

Fernando was a frank fellow, seldom restrained in conversation, especially when the topic of sex is raised. One day I addressed him point blank. "Look, Fernando, I know young people get together and make love before they are married. How do they do it?"

Fernando laughed and made a few obscene motions with his fists and arms. That stopped me for a moment. I wasn't accustomed to such graphic depictions. "No, you coyote. That's not what I mean. What I mean is, how do they manage to get together so that no one knows?"

He stared at me blankly.

"Look," I insisted, "There are ten people sleeping in the house. The girls never go alone to the bushes, the dogs bark at anybody who comes around. So how do they manage to pull it off without getting caught?"

Now Fernando became somewhat more serious, although he still had a fiendish gleam in his eye. "Well, they know each other you see. And they have agreed beforehand that he will visit her. Then in the middle of the night he comes to the part of the house where the dogs aren't and whispers for her. She whispers back and tells him where to come in. Everyone else is sound asleep and no one else knows."

"No one?"

Here he stopped and grinned. Maybe he was thinking about his own amorous escapades as a boy or of the times when he was awake and liaisons were taking place in the same area in which he was sleeping. Or, knowing Fernando, maybe my question had suggested to him the possibility that he could still get by with a little theft himself in spite of his forty years or so.

Anyway, I got no more information from him and to this day can't figure out how these secret affairs are carried on. I'm too much a coward to try to find out on the basis of personal experience. Maybe the answer is closer to what a crass North American, now dead, who knew the Seris well, told me. "It's easy. All you do is go out in the bushes and knock off a piece." Tersely stated.

The casual love affairs are, probably more than anything else, socially sanctioned play that can be taken care of should bad consequences result. I have not heard any talk among Seris of the value of virginity or the honor of women or other such marks of macho, male chauvinistic culture. Divorce is almost unheard of in Seri marriages, although cases are known where the union has not worked and the couple has split up. Once paired, almost all Seris bond for life, a far cry from the habits of the anthropologists whom they have seen over the years, who periodically show up with a different mate. Their family structure is very strong, yet not chauvinistically so. I often envied the strength of their family bonds.

Until recently, marriages were a simple affair, seldom attended by much ceremony. Increasingly though, Seris are adopting Mexican customs and having elaborate rituals, with tuxedos, gowns, musicians and all the other accouterments. One effect of this intrusion of Mexican culture is to have placed heavy economic demands on the families involved, forcing some to go into debt to pay for the elaborate ceremonies. The custom may not endure for it is not yet widespread. Yet the occurrence of only one or two such ceremonies has had a profound effect on Seri culture. Young people have begun to think of marriage in terms of glamour and romance. I think that alteration in rites of passage generally precedes alteration of the basic structures of a culture.

Young Seri women certainly spend a lot of time figuring out how to attract a mate. The Seris are a handsome race and the women are no exception. Tall and graceful, they begin to wear the traditional Seri dress, a long skirt and bordered blouse, at puberty. Their long, flowing hair is usually brushed vigorously, making it glisten in the desert sun.

One drawback is their teeth. I have already pointed out the wear and tear on women's teeth caused by preparing torote for basket making. Most Seris also have severe dental problems and in many cases poor teeth and gums detract from otherwise remarkable personal beauty. In young people it is both a health and a cosmetic problem. Whether it is because of the mottling of their teeth caused by excessive fluoride levels in their water, the enormous consumption of sugar and refined carbohydrates, their habits of using their teeth for general purpose tools (one child was known as "bottle-opener;" he took great delight in holding a soda pop bottle between his molars and removing the cap), genetic tendencies and a small gene pool or a combination of the above, few reach adulthood with attractive natural teeth. Seris also exhibit much gum disease, perhaps due to poor hygiene and diet, and many older women exhibit the torote-stripping syndrome.

Personal beauty, and the romantic traditions of marriage associated with it, however, seem to have a minor role to play in any decision to marry. *Novelas,* or soap opera novels, are becoming popular among young Seri women, but their cultural effects are not yet evident. Most of the decisions about matrimony are made by the parents who arrange the marriage and then also arrange for a bride price and payment.

The bride price is a bit of a problem, not only in that it can be abused, as in the case of José Astorga, but also because it means that a girl or young woman without a father to negotiate for her hand is in jeopardy of not finding a Seri mate. In one case, a lovely, talented woman had to wait until she was almost thirty before she married because she had no family to make the arrangements. When she finally found a mate, he treated her poorly and with the attitude that she should be thankful he would deign to marry her.

But they do marry and do beget children. As I've said, subtlety of lovemaking has to be a strongly developed art among them. Most are crowded into their huts or small houses in huge numbers—ten to a shack of a couple of rooms isn't unusual—and privacy is unknown.

Under these conditions, the night sounds can be hysterical or infuriating, depending upon how desperately one needs sleep. When all the snoring, sniffing, coughing and farting is combined with the restless movings of four or five dogs and as many cats, houses are hardly places of dignified repose at night. I found, on the few occasions I have slept in the houses, that sleep can be easier to come by during the day when the interior population is vastly decreased. I don't know how anybody can make love under those circumstances. On the other hand, throughout history, desperation has been known to lead ardent lovers to try anything.

One day I found that their marriages are no freer of problems than marriages in our own culture. I was sitting in the yard of a family, watching the carving and basket making which were going on. For one reason or

another, those who were sitting around left, one by one, and after a while
I was left alone with a Seri woman in her mid-thirties. (An unusual
circumstance, as Seri women seldom are left alone with any outsider,
particularly a man.)

Feeling a bit awkward, I struck up a conversation with her, not a simple
thing because Spanish does not come easy for most Seri women. She soon
cut out the small talk, however.

"Daveed, I don't know what to do."

"What is the problem?" I inquired.

"My husband (I knew them both) doesn't love me."

"Oh, yes he does." I assured her. "He is just like so many men who have
a hard time expressing themselves."

"No, he doesn't. He told me so and I don't know what to do."

I was rescued by the return of some of the family members and, much
to my relief, the conversation was never resumed. I had a hard enough time
facing my own problems, much less giving advice to the lovelorn among the
Seris.

Radical feminists wouldn't find much regarding the division of labor among
the Seris about which to wax enthusiastic. Men spend a lot of time lying
around and chewing the fat as if they were waiting for something. Women
almost always seem to be working. Division of labor is sharp and
uncompromising. Men fish, hunt and carve. Women cook, do laundry, tend
to children, weave baskets and carve. Generally men carve the basic figure
and women do the fine finishing with sandpaper and wax. Although many
women, including some of the best artists, also carve, I have never seen
women carve while men do the finishing on a regular basis. When I asked
Angelita Torres if any women ever fish, she giggled as if I were asking if
women ever pole vault. My questions about men's involvement in basket
making were met with embarrassed smiles.

And yet Seri women are frequently strong and independent. They are
proud of being known as artists in their own right. They, not their husbands,
set the prices for their own work. Frequently husbands are the salesmen,
but must consult with their wives about an offer.

Seri men do not appear to be cursed with a need to express themselves as machos, although to some extent I find this trait to be increasingly evident among younger men, a fact Jim Hills has suggested corresponds with the proliferation of pickup trucks.

A year or so after I was divorced I was speaking with Chalió Astorga, José's middle son, a superb carver and talented musician. He was curious about the circumstances of my divorce and expressed dismay that my wife and I were no longer together.

"Daveed," he began, assuming a rather paternalistic tone for one ten years younger than I, "You need to come down here and marry a Seri girl."

"Why should I do that? Women can bring a lot of grief."

"But with Seri girls it is different. Here they aren't like they are in other places. Other women do bad things and embarrass their husbands. Not so with Seri girls."

Then Chalió, who has a Mexican wife, really got to the point. He looked at me, noting that I was skinny and dressed as most North Americans dress. "What you need to do is get some cowboy boots, grow your hair long and learn to walk with your chest stuck out. And you need to wear a hat."

So far I haven't taken his advice.

Seris consider Mexicans to be without shame. Mexicans consider gringos to be without shame. So the reader can image what the Seris must think of North Americans. They think we are congenial barbarians who are fortunate to be rich. And yet they have their own myths about our sexuality, one of which is that North American men have enormous penises. I am unable to document the origin of this belief.

An incident concerning Gonzalo Astorga, José's youngest son, feeds the mythology that we have no shame. In the late 1960s I took my family and Joan, my older sister to Desemboque. We camped a mile or so north of town in an area where a few sand dunes gave some protection against the cold northwest wind.

One morning after a chilly and damp night, the sun came out warm and bright, promising to heat the area into the seventies. I had some business

Nora Molina

in town so I took the Land Rover in, telling the women that I would be gone for a couple of hours.

Patsy and Joan decided that it was time for them to take advantage of the warm sun. With only our young children around, what could be more natural and invigorating than a nice sun bath, a time of langour in which the sun's gentle rays could caress their lithe bodies with its sensuous magnificence? This was, after all, the sixties. In short, they stripped and lay out on towels and cots in the sun, oblivious to the rest of the world, which must have seemed remote.

Gonzalo was a nice young man of thirteen or fourteen at the time. He was one of the few Seris who owned a bicycle and he was constantly riding it. While I was in town he decided to hop on his bicycle and visit our camp, perhaps intending to deliver a message to me. After lying on the cot in the broad sunlight for a while, Patsy remembered something that she needed from the tent. She got up and walked toward the tent, blissfully naked. There, standing on his bike, was an astonished Gonzalo. Patsy hastily grabbed a towel and threw some clothes to Joan who prudently and deftly managed to cover her body.

Gonzalo was not to be deterred. He smilingly went over to Patsy, informing her that his father wished to speak with me, got back on his bike and headed back to town.

When I returned to camp, Patsy and Joan were still giggling. They related the story with great zest, amazed at the degree of aplomb that Gonzalo had demonstrated. I was very curious to see just what Gonzalo would have to say about it.

Later that day I had occasion to go back into town and visit the Astorgas. Gonzalo seemed to be studiously avoiding me. So I brashly yelled out, "Hey, Gonzalo, what did you see out at my camp?" He peered out of the house, not knowing whether I was angry or not. He saw me grinning from ear to ear.

"Nothing," he mumbled.

The place exploded with laughter.

"¿No vió nada?" I asked facetiously. (You didn't see anything at all?)

"No ví nada." (I didn't see anything), he said with a silly, embarrassed expression.

Then Santiago, Gonzalo's eldest brother, laughed out loud. "No vió nada," he roared. (He didn't see anything.)

After that Gonzalo had a new name. And to this day I still tease him and call him "No vió nada."

I have often wondered just what erotic fantasies preoccupied the youth after his brief encounter with the amazing world of liberated North American women.

Change in mores has come to the Seris. I was astonished, upon taking a Seri woman and her brother to a dentist in Hermosillo, to see her remove her Seri skirt while she was inside the Rover. Underneath she wore a pair of blue jeans. I fear that it is only a matter of time before bathing suits and suntan oil find their way to Desemboque.

Stingrays

"Estrike dos." (Strike two.) The count was full, runners on first and third, two out.

I was umpiring a baseball game. Not softball, baseball. A couple of the young men had stopped by our ramada and asked me to umpire. It was a lovely summer evening and the living was easy, a perfect time for a baseball game. At first I was honored, thinking they must have respected me to ask me to umpire. Then I realized that they all wanted to play and no one wanted to be umpire, so my self-esteem dropped a couple of notches.

I readily agreed, however, and walked behind home plate on the bare, sandy field located on the east side of the village. I quickly found that it was no sandlot game of baseball. A couple of the young men were excellent baseball players and one was a terrific pitcher. (I once had ten swings at his pitches and finally gave up in disgust after hitting nothing but air.)

As it turned out, my verdicts were important, for the players really cared who won the game. Once, on a two-and-two count the pitch was so close I couldn't bring myself to pronounce it either a ball or a strike. I looked quickly around and saw a dozen or so grimly expectant faces staring at me. Given my proximity to the pitcher, I made the prudent choice and called the pitch a strike. The batter was out.

Now, with a three-and-two count there was a bit of excitement, for the score was close and it was getting dark. The pitcher wound up and set, when I heard a scream. I whirled around and saw my son Chris riding on the back of a young Seri's bicycle, shrieking. I ran toward him and saw that his foot was caught in the spokes. By the time I reached him he had extricated his foot. I grabbed him in my arms as he sobbed. As the Seris watched I examined his foot. It was red and had a small abrasion, but wasn't broken or sprained. I began to be ashamed that my own flesh and blood could not tolerate pain any better. My son was going to be more manly than that.

I scolded him mildly, in Spanish, for their benefit.

"Come on, Chris, it isn't anything at all."

Campuzano was standing nearby. He reminded me sternly, "Daveed, it hurts him." As Chris continued to sob, I realized Campuzano was right. Suitably chastized, I more appropriately comforted my little boy.

They never did finish the game. It was called on account of darkness.

Chris was six at the time we were spending a couple of weeks in Desemboque. Towheaded, green-eyed and fair skinned, he was a textbook example of a gringo boy. He was a village favorite, a familiar sight to the Seris who seemed quite fond of him, and generally welcome in their simple huts, timid though he was about entering them. Many times I saw them tentatively touching his hair and skin, marvelling at the quirk of nature that could produce such a strange and potentially unhealthy color in a child, perhaps pitying Patsy and me, his parents, for having a child of such an odd hue.

As with all outsiders with whom they become familiar, they gave Chris a name. "Arrios Cocazhni," they called him. Arrios means nothing at all, but was the closest he could come to saying adios. Each time he saw someone walking by he would yell "Arrios!" "Cocazhni" is the Seri word for sidewinder. It was also just about the only Seri word that Chris could remember, even after spending lots of time playing with Seri children his age. The village people picked up on his linguistic peculiarity and attached the name to him.

Their system of name giving is simple: each child is given a name based upon the first recognizable sound the child makes. Frequently babies a year old still have no names. Once a name is given, it becomes their Seri name and sticks with them until they reach puberty. After that it is dropped, or, at least not publicly used, for it is thought to be impolite to use a child's name for an adult.

Historically, the Seris did not bear names as they do now and after puberty they were referred to simply by description, such as "The second son of the man whose father died in the spring," or "The woman whose son dances in the morning." It was a system that worked fine with a small group but would provide interesting confusion with a larger population.

Fortunately for us (and, I think for them), they readily adopted the Spanish system of names, so now every child is also sooner or later given a Spanish name. When women marry, they do not take the name of their husband, a refreshing improvement on our male-dominated system.

Seris have been known to take on the entire name of a respected outsider. Three notable examples are Roberto Thomson, named after a Mexican who, in the earlier part of this century, befriended the Seris and became a powerful advocate for them; Pancho Hoeffer, named after a German fisherman; and Miguel Barnet, whose family has prospered and whose son, Chapo I have already described, and who bears the name of an old Mexican family.

The Seris also give descriptive names to outsiders, labels which are seldom flattering. Ed Moser, who spent more than twenty-five years in the village was called "Turtle Head" (a surprisingly accurate description). Becky was named "Woman Who Sings," as nice a Seri name as I have heard. A North American trader who frequently bought carvings and baskets was called "Messy Hair," another, "Hair Tied in a Bob." Jim Hills was called "Crazy Jim." I was given the dubious label, "Father of the Black Dog," a clear indication of who they deemed most significant in my family.

Chris has not been back to Desemboque since he underwent puberty. If he were to return, he would probably no longer be called "Arrios Cocazhni" since the name was attached to him when he was quite young, but he would be given a descriptive name. Someday he will go back and it will be interesting to see what label they attach to him.

There was a good deal of consternation among the more responsible parents when I allowed Chris to play in the ocean in front of our ramada. It's not that Seri children don't play in the ocean—it's just that because of stingrays they seldom proceed more than a few feet from the water's edge.

Indeed, before the advent of plastic toys and boats, most young boys had a hand-made boat which they learned to push expertly along the edge of the tide with a stick inserted in the bow, always managing to avoid water more than ankle deep, yet keeping the boat in the water. I purchased a couple of these boats, handcarved from elephant tree wood, and my children spent many happy hours playing with them in the ocean and in Arizona streams. Unhappily for us, they were one day washed away by an Arizona flash flood. Who knows, perhaps they made their way down the Gila River to the Colorado and through the Colorado Delta into the Gulf of California and washed ashore in their ancestral home. At one time I thought about encouraging the Seris to make the boats for sale, for they are so captivating. I gave up on the idea, however, when I realized that mass production would lead to extermination of the elephant trees from which they are made.

In the Seri portion of the Gulf of California an abundance of stingrays are found. These insidious beasts, seldom more than eighteen inches long, are very dangerous due to their highly potent sting and their nasty habit of burying themselves in the sand at the ocean's bottom, where they can't be seen. When stepped on, the stingrays instantly respond with a flick of the razor-sharp stinger located at the base of the spine. The apparatus easily penetrates the flesh, usually leaving a deep cut, bad enough in itself, but made worse by a powerful venom which produces a sting or ache as potent as virtually any pain-causing substance I know of. Most Seris who have also been bitten by a rattlesnake (all Seri Men have scars to demonstrate their stings) swear the sting of a ray is more painful than the bite of a rattlesnake. The pain works itself up the leg and causes a powerful throbbing in the lymph glands in the groin area, making one wish for swift last rites and burial.

Even worse in the long run, is the fact that the stinger provides a nice habitat for an obscure fungus which can infect the wound, preventing healing. I recall an older North American couple who were once camped near us on the Gulf. The husband ventured out barefoot into the surf and was promptly stung by a ray. In his agony he applied ice to the wound, one of the worst things he could have done. (As I later learned, ice is probably the worst thing you can put on a stingray injury—almost as bad as putting ice on a rattlesnake bite.) The next day he said it felt better, but we later learned that his wound refused to heal. After some months he was forced

Seri men carrying caguama—wary of stingrays

to undergo surgery to excise the infected area. Don't mess around with stingrays.

Chris knew all about stingrays, having watched Seri young men spear them from their boats, impaling them on the barbed points of the effective harpoons they carry with them while fishing. It is an easy recreation for the boys to make a game of seeing how many stingrays they can catch while waiting for a boat to be loaded for a fishing trip. They hold the harpoon over the water till they see the characteristic imprint the stingrays make on the bottom. Then they spear with a quick thrust and bring the impaled creature wriggling out of the water. In spite of this sport and the huge numbers of rays removed from the depths by it, their numbers seem hardly phased. I suspect that modern fishing has somehow removed a predator from the Gulf, allowing the number of rays to proliferate. They are a menace, rendering dangerous huge expanses of beach along the Gulf.

As a modern parent, I was eagerly allowing my children freedom to experience their environment. I was also prudent. I required Chris to wear tennis shoes when he was playing in the surf. No way a ray's sting can penetrate a shoe, my wife and I agreed. The Seris never allow their youngsters to play out as far as Chris was, except to dive from boats, since their children are generally not good swimmers. Chris was an excellent swimmer, and protected by his shoes, was having a marvelous time with a styrofoam surfboard.

His sudden screams put an end to his playtime for the day. I didn't hesitate. I ran, fully dressed, into the Gulf and gathered him into my arms. The water was little more than waist-deep and there wasn't much surf, so I was able quite quickly to deposit him back on the shore.

"My foot, my foot," he screamed. It was not difficult to see. There, slightly above the ball of his foot, was a hole in the shoe with a river of blood flowing through. So much for my complacent theory that shoes will protect against stingrays. His screams summoned help far more quickly than my calls could have. Nor was it necessary for me to explain "Le picó manta." Everyone knew what had happened.

Fortunately, they also knew exactly what to do. Over the centuries Seris have learned, through trial and error, to prepare cures for the thousands of ray stings they have experienced. Since ice was not available until recent decades, their remedies never included ice.

The Indians didn't seem to be in a hurry to end Chris's agony. Rather soon an older woman, Lupe Herrera, appeared and told me to build a fire. I asked if my Coleman stove would be all right and she, somewhat disdainfully, assented. Soon two of her daughters appeared, each carrying a different herb, one of which was torote, the very plant from which baskets are made. Two flat rocks were produced. She ordered me to begin to put water on to boil as she undertook most deliberately to grind the weeds on the stones.

It seemed an eternity before the water was hot enough, but it was really only a few minutes. I pumped the stove like a madman, hoping I could induce the water to boil more quickly. When it began to bubble, Lupe tossed a couple of bunches of both herbs, well crushed, into the water and let them stew. Meanwhile, Chris's screaming continued unabated and I wanted to hide somewhere so as not to see my son in agony.

Then, with practiced dignity, she carefully placed a kerchief over the wound and with a large cloth, began to dribble the hot brew, somewhat cooled, over the wound. The cloths were a good idea, since they provided some protection against burning the skin and also distributed the liquid well while helping to retain the heat. Lupe ordered me to boil more water. I thought Chris would not pull through. For the next two hours Chris continued to have horrible pain. Lupe, without much expression but with deep compassion and years of experience, comforted him in the graceful Seri way, while she continued to apply the hot liquid to the wound.

Suddenly his screams ceased. He started to smile and gave a nervous giggle. "Daddy, it doesn't hurt anymore," he exclaimed.

Lupe rose, gave me a knowing smile and walked back to her hut. I ordered Chris not to move and took over the application of the tea. But there was no need, no need at all. Everyone knew the cure was complete.

I looked at the wound. It was hardly visible, although there had been a deep gash a couple of hours earlier. Chris wanted to get up and walk around and began to laugh and chatter. No responsible parent would permit such a thing. No, young man, you have been severely injured and must remain recumbent, I thought. I, your father, know better than these barbarians. The Seris must have known what I was thinking and doing. The younger ones looked at me as though I were slightly daft and wandered away looking for more interesting things to do than watch a weird foreigner mistreat his son. Crazy gringos!

Chris went to sleep early that night, exhausted by his ordeal with pain. I was worried about infection and resolved to repeat the treatment in the morning. At sunup he was awake and I examined the wound again. Hardly a mark. No redness or swelling. Not even tender to the touch. Well, I would ask Lupe.

She was less than helpful. When I asked her if I should repeat the treatment she looked at me as though I had asked her if she were a jet pilot. She had provided her cure and that was that. What more did I want, miracles? Without her having to say a word, she had communicated her message to me rather lucidly.

Chris felt no more pain, nor was there ever any sign of infection. A month later there was not even a discernible scar. The wound never gave him the slightest problem.

Some time later I read that new evidence showed the best treatment for stings from a stingray is hot water. The pain-producing toxin is serotonin, which is broken down by heat. The application of ice helps prevent breakdown of the serotonin and may lead to infection. Smart bunch, we with our sophisticated technology that provides medical breakthroughs.

Two or three years later I was walking around barefoot in the Gulf when I felt a dagger enter my foot. It was a stingray. Luckily for me, a couple of Seri women nearby had been trying to sell me a basket. They immediately went into action and produced the required herbs. Although the wound was ferociously painful, I was relaxed, knowing I was in the best medical hands. Sure enough, two hours later the pain ceased, never to reappear. I couldn't even point to a scar a month later. Primitive folks, these Seris.

At this point I still hadn't learned that Seris almost never do anything for free, that a return favor or gift is always expected when a favor or service is rendered. Several years after Chris's sting it occurred to me that I had not given anything to Lupe in return for her having "cured" Chris. I resolved to remedy this ancient wrong. So in 1983, more than thirteen years after the incident, I saw Lupe walking by and resolved to take care of my debt to her. I approached her.

"Lupe, do you remember when you cured my son Chris of the sting of a ray?"

"Aahssah," she nodded. Her broad smile, changing her usually impassive face, revealed that she remembered well.

"Well, I failed to give you something for curing him, didn't I?"

"Aahssah," she nodded emphatically, "you did forget."

Having no other gift available, I gave her a nice sum of money. She smiled approvingly, looked at me deeply for an instant and went on her way, undoubtedly marvelling at the mysterious insanity that bedevils gringos.

San Esteban

No Seris wanted to go. Even though the boat was a Seri boat, everyone, even Chapo, had something more important to do than take a trip to San Esteban Island.

We should have been more perceptive. We should have taken heed. But we weren't and we didn't.

Jim Hills, my brother Dick, and I had been itching for years to go to San Esteban. Now we had the time, the boat, and the opportunity. As traders, we were able to place our myriad orders, leave for a few days then come back and pick up the merchandise. It was January and the weather was great. There would be no jejenes and it would be cool enough so we could hike comfortably on the island.

San Esteban lies in the Gulf of California, southwest of Isla Tiburón. The two islands are separated by a deep channel ten miles wide, notorious for treacherous currents. A small island, San Esteban has an area of little more than ten square miles and a fairly reliable supply of fresh water. It is historically important for the Seris because it lies midway between the mainland and the coast of Baja California and hence provided a good stopping place for them on fishing expeditions.

Why did we want to go there? First, I suppose, because it is an island, a real desert island which holds the lure islands seem to hold for mainlanders. And San Esteban is unique, geologically, botanically and zoologically. The island peaks rise nearly 2000 feet. It has never been grazed by livestock and, because its mammalian population does not include predators, being limited to small rodents, a peculiar lizard has managed to evolve and fill a special ecological niche.

The San Esteban chuckwalla *(Sauromalus saurus)* is a large, iguana-like lizard found nowhere else in the world. Up to two feet in length, it is valued as food by the Seris who importuned us to bring some back for them. We wouldn't, though, for the lizard is a truly endangered species.

San Esteban also has a large population of sea lions. These huge beasts seem to prefer the security and isolation of San Esteban to other islands in the area. They find the abundant fish in that part of the Gulf very much to their liking.

But it was more because San Esteban had been the home, decades ago, of a band of Seris, that we wanted to go. If the Seris had lived there, we reasoned, it must be a fine place. We were determined to visit the island, remote though it might be.

Jim had scrounged around and located an old Seri plank boat in Punta Chueca, bought it from its owner, painted it and filled most of the numerous holes, and proceeded, along with its former owner, to pronounce it seaworthy. The boat was big and heavy, large enough for a good ten people if necessary, but just about right for three men and their supplies for five days. He also located a 10-horsepower motor for the trip, had it tuned, rounded up some gas tanks and got a few suggestions for the trip from the Seris (several of whom, I now realize, considered us utterly mad). Dick and I flew to Hermosillo from Tucson. Jim picked us up at the airport and we drove to Punta Chueca that night.

Our trappings made a pile several feet high on the beach. "God, what a bunch of crap!" Jim observed. It took us most of the next morning to pack the boat with this embarrassing load—water, ice chests, gasoline, food, blankets, clothes and sleeping bags. We were hardened wilderness adventurers, but needed *some* comforts after all. The Seris, accustomed to traveling with only the most spartan provisions, watched with a mixture of amusement, tinged with envy and incredulity, as we piled in our mountain of possessions.

Finally we were ready. The Seris gave us a few parting words as they helped push off. Some were watching wonderingly and as I look back I think a few of them even had expressions of concern—especially the former owner of the boat.

The winds were calm as we took off. No sooner had we left the small harbor, however, when we discovered we had a problem. The motor was too small and the drive shaft too short for the size of the boat. When we reached the top of a swell and the prow headed down the other side, the propeller would clear the surface of the water, racing badly and leaving the boat totally without power. Since a boat motor is water-cooled, removal from the cooling water for only a short time can cause the motor to overheat. We alleviated this problem somewhat by shifting most of our supplies toward the back of the boat, a major effort which made the prow ride rather high in the water so we looked like a floating check mark on the horizon. But at least we were able to keep the propeller in the water most of the time.

Looking over our situation, Jim, as captain of the ship, decided the safest way to navigate would be to keep a low speed. We proceeded at less than ten knots, certainly a speed at which we could revel in the marvels of the Gulf, but not one which would wing us rapidly toward our destination, almost fifty miles away.

We had planned to check in at the marine garrison directly across the Infernillo from Punta Chueca, assuming it was necessary to obtain permission to camp on Tiburón as we planned. But we had been so delayed and our progress would be so slow that Jim decided to head due south and forego the extra hour or so it would have taken to stop at the garrison and obey the rumored regulation.

We settled down for a long ride. The water was now smooth and as we made our way along the shore of Isla Tiburón it was a thrill to see this massive preserve much as the ancient Seris had beheld it, with its geological marvels of volcanic cones and rugged, faulted uplifts.

We learned quickly about the boat. Stopping for lunch at a beach, we hopped out on the sand, after dropping anchor, paying little attention to the ebbing tide. We were snoozing on the beach when I awoke to see the boat wobbling in the water. It was about to be beached by the outgoing tide. I woke Jim and Dick and we frantically raced out to push the boat farther out in the water. This sounds simple, but it was no easy task with a boat that weighed more than a ton. Just when I thought we would be stranded for the next ten hours, a small wave lifted the boat free and we were able to push it into deeper water.

This experience presented us with a dilemma: if we brought the boat up far enough on the beach so we could wade to shore, we stood a good chance of having it beached by the tide, which is all right if you plan to stay for twelve hours, no more and no less; if we left it out far enough to guarantee it would be free of the tide's tricks, we would have to wade in and out each time, get thoroughly soaked, and have difficulty loading and unloading our trappings, to say nothing of the hazard from stingrays. From all of this though, we learned to choose our landing sites with more caution.

The motor droned on as the afternoon waned. We rounded the southern tip of Isla Tiburón and decided to head for Turner Island for the night. Turner is a small isle, probably no more than a few hundred acres in size, not far off Tiburón's southern extremity. As we crossed the channel the wind picked up, making a welcome sight of what appeared to be a beach. As we neared it however, we discovered it was so steep that camping would be impossible, meaning we would have to return to Tiburón. It was almost sundown and swells were developing, so the ride back across the channel was tense. When we reached the coast of Tiburón we encountered either cliffs or steep slopes where we could not anchor the boat and camp.

It was now we began to realize how important it is to have a sufficiently powerful motor. With the sun beginning to set, no prospect of camp in sight, and the swells still increasing, we faced the bleak prospect of spending the night on the boat, drifting. Our little motor was not capable of delivering the speed or power necessary to get us quickly to an adequate camping spot.

Then, as we rounded another point on Tiburón, we entered a calm bay with a beach that sloped gradually, ideal for us to make our camp. We hurriedly anchored and dragged our load up on the shore, thankful to be off the water and watching the sun set. We were not the first to take refuge in this cove, we discovered. On the dunes above the beach we found remnants of former Seri camps and even some potsherds indicating that it had been a haven for ancient inhabitants of the island as well.

Early the next morning we were off. The Gulf was calmer than it had been on the previous night. We headed west by northwest following the coast of Isla Tiburón, toward a point straight across from San Esteban where the channel is narrowest and where we would undertake the crossing. Before we had gone far, however, we passed a building barely visible on the shore from which a signal flashed. The Seris had mentioned another marine garrison on the southern end of the island. It appeared the marines were ordering us in.

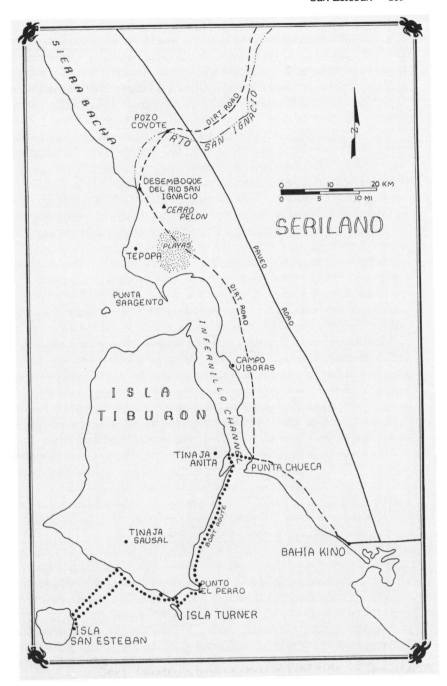

Seri country showing route of boat ride in January, 1981

We debated for a few minutes as to the wisest course. We could ignore the flash, and if overtaken by patrol boats, feign ignorance. Or we could head toward the garrison, with the risk that we would be told we couldn't land on Tiburón or San Esteban. The flashing became more urgent. We headed in. Our small boat with its pathetic motor could never evade a patrol boat.

The garrison was a paltry affair with only a small, derelict pier and a corrugated metal shack. We docked and fastened the boat. The marines were friendly. They were just playing with their signal mirror, they joked. Jim joked also and handed them a bottle of rotgut whiskey he had brought for just such a situation. They accepted it eagerly. Military life on this outpost of civilization can get pretty boring. No, they said, there would be no problem if we wanted to stay on the island or on San Esteban. Just be careful in the channel, they warned. Bad currents.

After a few minutes more of small talk, we hopped back in the boat and continued up the coast of Tiburón, passing under towering cliffs where the relentless action of the ocean had sheared away huge slices of rock. When our charts showed us to be at the narrowest point of the channel, we set out for San Esteban, which loomed gray and blue in the distance.

Our progress was excruciatingly slow. I became tense as the swells grew and whitecaps began to appear. The motor, which now seemed only a plaything, regularly popped out of the water and raced, only to labor when it re-entered the ocean. Ahead a whale breached, sending up a geyser of spray from its blowhole, but we were too preoccupied to enjoy the amazing spectacle. Farther ahead yet we could see an increasing number of whitecaps as we left the lee of Tiburón and entered the open ocean.

About halfway across, we glimpsed the current which runs between the two islands. It was a relief to see the current, for we had heard stories about its ferocity and deceptiveness. At last we were taking it on and it did not appear so bad. It was marked by small waves and water of a different color, but no giant whirlpools. We would have loved to avoid it, but we had no choice. We had to cross it to get to San Esteban.

The boat lurched to portside as we hit the current. The motor labored even more and Jim had to struggle with the rudder to keep the craft on course. The sea was downright rough and spray blew in our faces as the current, combined with a quickening wind, splashed the waves against the bow. It was cold and getting colder. We huddled down as far as possible in the boat. Each time we struck a wave, Dick and I had to bail out the water that poured in over the edge. As we bailed and I cursed under my breath, my admiration increased greatly for the old Seris who made this crossing repeatedly in their reed boats. Then quite suddenly, after only a quarter of an hour, we were out of the current and in calmer water. The swells decreased and our speed picked up. We slowly relaxed and watched as we approached San Esteban.

A mile or so off the island we picked up the lee and the water became smoother still. We reached a point a quarter mile from the cliffs where we could make out individual plants on the land and headed south.

At the first cove we stopped and stared, amazed at the spectacle. Dozens of sea lions were sunning themselves on the rocks. Some of their number had seen us and dived into the water. Before long their heads reappeared above the surface as they swam in our direction. They stopped about fifty yards away, remaining stationary in the water with their heads sticking out, gazing at us with what looked like a mixture of curiosity and hope. If we were fishermen, they knew we might share our bounty with them. We moved on slowly, enchanted by the sea lions and the wild cliffs of the island, knowing that making our camp would be a chore for which we were in no hurry.

San Esteban has but one beach, if it can be called that, on its east side. When we arrived there it took us several minutes to find the best place to anchor. Much to our dismay, we found the bottom of the cove to be covered with large rocks and boulders so the boat could not reach the shore. Our only alternative was to drop anchor a couple of hundred feet from the water's edge and carry our gear through the knee-deep water. Transporting our supplies over the slippery boulders was a hazard and on one trip Dick slipped and fell. But the water was calm and beautiful and not too cold, so the job was not unpleasant. The old Seris had it all over us. Their balsas were so bouyant they required only a few inches of water to float. They would have been able to reach the shore without wading.

The rest of the day we spent exploring. The chuckwallas were there, although not so numerous as I had hoped. We hiked into the interior, noting in several places signs of old Seri camps. We found no permanent water, only a couple of rain-filled pot-holes a mile and a half from the beach. The birds were numerous, the plant life exotic and the steep mountains majestic.

Evening arrived soon and we prepared for the night. As darkness set in a few wisps of clouds from the west blew over the tops of the peaks. Being on the eastern side of the island, we could not see the sunset or the weather in the west, where winter storms come from.

As we prepared to climb into our sleeping bags, it struck me that the night was very dark. I thought for a moment and it hit me. There was no moon. We were in the new moon, the time when the spring tides are highest in the Gulf. No wonder the Seris had looked uneasy when we departed! The currents are worst during spring tides. They are bad enough during neap tides, treacherous during spring tides. We were lucky to have arrived safely, but tomorrow the tides would be higher and if a storm was coming, higher yet. I tried not to think about it and fell asleep.

Just before dawn I awoke to the sensation of raindrops on my face. Dick and Jim awoke at the same time. Jim heard the sound of the boat hitting on a rock from time to time as it thrashed around on its moorings. That meant the bay was no longer calm, but choppy. A wind had sprung up with the rain. Jim trotted off through the dark and waded out to check the boat. I was glad he was doing it and not I. I felt clammy inside my down sleeping bag.

Winter storms in the Gulf are seldom brief. They tend to be part of large cyclonic weather systems that move west to east out of the Pacific, often lingering for several days, stalled by mountain ranges or high pressure weather centers to the east. They can cause heavy rains and high seas in Gulf regions. Most of all they cause unceasing northwest winds that grow cold as they blow across the Gulf of California.

Jim felt it was urgent that we leave. We had water enough for only one day and precious little food. If a three-day storm should strike we could be in trouble.

It was chilly and the water felt downright cold as we slipped over boulders carrying our gear out to the boat, barely visible in the pre-dawn glow. Jim had discovered a large hole in the side of the boat where it had been banging on a rock and had repaired it the best he could, but we could see that water was still pouring into the bottom. From time to time a brief rainshower pelted us. The clouds were gathering darker and darker along the mountain peaks to the west of us in the direction from which the storm was coming.

Jim and Dick worked like Trojans. I puttered around, hoping Jim might change his mind and stay on the island. I would prefer taking my chances on the island without water, than with the angry seas we would have to cross to reach Tiburón. But Jim was captain and he was determined. He pulled up the anchor. We pushed the boat out to the deeper water, getting thoroughly wet in the process, and piled into the damp boat. Jim fired up the motor and headed the bow to the east. I burrowed into the hull.

We were barely out of the tiny bay in which we had anchored when we found that the swells were even bigger than on the previous day. The wind was brisk out of the north, meaning we would have to cross the channel parallel to the swells, risking being capsized. Some troughs between the waves were so deep we could not see Isla Tiburón until we crested on the next swell. And we were still within the lee of the island.

I held on tightly to the seat of the boat shivering from the cold and from fear. Dick's face was grim as he rode amidships. At the motor, Jim grimaced as the icy spray blew in his face and the boat rocked in the rough water. The impossibly small motor alternately raced and labored as the stern rocked in and out of the water. We were only a half mile or so from San Esteban, nine and a half miles from Tiburón and safety.

Then we emerged from the lee. The wind shook the boat, forcing the bow to the south. Jim struggled to keep on course. The waves increased in size and one broke over the side of the boat. Water poured in faster than Dick and I could bail. Jim had to hang on with one hand and guide the rudder with the other. I knew we couldn't possibly survive the crossing. And the worst was still to come for we hadn't yet arrived at the current. I looked back at Jim. Without giving any word, he turned the boat around in a broad circle and we headed back to San Esteban. I saw the color returning to Dick's face. I don't know whether the tears on my face were from fear or from the spray.

A half hour later we were back in the cove, carrying our gear onto the beach. It was sprinkling and we were damp, but it was dry land. I looked back over the angry waters. I don't know why I hadn't demanded to stay from the first. I guess it was my macho streak. But now we were safe. We found a small cave in a hillside above the wash where we had camped. Throwing our blankets on the ground we slept like dead men.

When I awoke a couple of hours later, Jim and Dick were still asleep. Most of the clouds were gone and the sun had come out, but the wind was still stiff out of the north and the ocean to the east was covered with angry whitecaps. There would be no escape from San Esteban that day, water or no water. I checked our supply. I found about two quarts left, plus one six-pack of beer. Enough for one man, but surely not for three. We could, of course, boil sea water and distill it, but I doubted we could do that efficiently enough to provide water for the three of us.

I picked up our canteens and water bottles and began to hike inland up the wash to where it became a canyon and forked. I took the north fork and hiked another mile or so. After a long search I found the water-filled pot-holes which we had discovered the day before. They contained perhaps four gallons of the precious liquid. Although there were numerous signs of animal activity around the holes, the water appeared to be clean enough.

I took my tin cup, carefully dipped water from the depressions and poured it into the canteens. I managed to fill both canteens this way while still leaving water for the local waterhole crowd. I would hate to have been the efficient cause of the extermination of an as yet undiscovered rare and endangered species dependent on that particular source of water for its survival.

I trudged back to our camp and triumphantly deposited the replenished water supply in front of my comrades. Jim laughed and produced a large bottle of water with several gallons in it, a bottle that had been almost empty a couple of hours earlier. Then he told me that he and Dick had gone exploring on the other side of the cove and found a barrel of water some fishermen must have hidden in a crevice in a rock face as an emergency supply for occasions just like this. I felt a lot of resentment towards those anonymous souls who with their foresight had rendered insignificant a heroic and noble act on my part. But I would be damned if I was going to walk almost two miles back up the wash and re-deposit in the pot-holes the water I had brought down in such a dedicated fashion.

The next day dawned clear and calm. The crossing was routine, although the hole in the side of the boat leaked enough to keep Dick and me busy bailing. The waves were barely a foot high and the wind was only a slight land breeze which kept the heat down. When we reached Isla Tiburón it was as though we were home safe and sound. We shared our camp with the memories of countless generations of Seris who had made this part of the island their permanent home because of available water and abundant fish in the channel between the two islands.

We spent that day hiking up to a carrizo on the west side where we found ample water, enough to swim in and the only running water in all of Seri country. The path was littered along its entire length with shards from pots which didn't quite make the arduous journey from the tinajas to the camp.

Early the following morning we set off for Punta Chueca. I was tense most of the trip back, fearing that the wind would spring up, as is often the case in the cool months. I held my breath as we rounded Punto El Perro, the southern tip of Isla Tiburón. If the winds were going to catch us, it would be here out of the lee of the island. But luck was with us and the ocean remained calm. Around noon we saw the water tower of Punta Chueca and soon the huts also came into view.

The village had for me all the comforts of a metropolis, a cosmopolitan center of affluence and culture, so relieved was I to be back from a battle with the sea. Antonio Topete's little store was a supermarket. The ironwood vendors comprised an international bazaar.

We were greeted by a curious crowd of Seris. They told us later they had been concerned about us and were prepared to send a search party had we not returned on that day. I suppose they hadn't advised us against leaving for San Esteban when we did out of diplomacy or perhaps because it is not considered polite by Seris to render advice unless it is requested.

To this day, the Seris tell the story, first related by Jim, that Daveed was so scared in the boat that he cried. I've never figured out how to set the record straight. Try as I may to explain that the wind was blowing in my face and I was really only tense, my defenses are only interpreted as further proof of my weakness. I guess that is part of the evaluation the Seris have made of me. Daveed really is a weak man.

Never mind that I have kayaked in places they would never go, have demonstrated to them how to handle snakes, have shown that I could outrun their most stalwart youth, have taught them a good deal about nutrition and medicine, have blithely picked up tarantulas in their presence, have shown them how to take apart and reassemble a chain saw; it is all for naught. Jim's story fixed me for good.

Night

Night affects different folks differently. Some people live only for night. Others succumb to its irresistable invitation to sleep.

The Seris, like rural folk everywhere, are among the latter. It might be different for those who live beyond the 30th parallels north and south, where the length of day and night vary greatly. In the extreme northern and southern regions the long winter nights necessitate adaption to darkness and stimulate outdoor activities in the absence of the sun.

For the Seris, nine o'clock marks the end of most activity. After ten o'clock almost no one is awake. Even then, the generator, on the few occasions when it manages to roar into life and provide electricity, shuts down early. Candles and portable lanterns flicker and are gone. A few dogs bark randomly and without conviction and silence gradually extends its peaceful hand over the face of the earth.

Not always so, just almost always. A puberty festival for a young woman may last all night. During these uncommon rites, marathon pascola dances release previously untested stores of energy, maintaining the participants for up to thirty-six hours nonstop.

More typically, New Year's Eve, a celebration imported from the U.S., along with the ironwood revolution, is observed only by a few pseudodionysiac revellers. The feeble lights of the village barely penetrate the overwhelming presence of night. The atmosphere is not one of carnival. One winter evening I was sitting by a campfire at the Astorgas' house. A lot of people were milling around at what I thought would be everyone's usual bedtime. A couple of the younger Seri women had city-type skirts on, not their Seri dresses. What was going on, I asked. They looked at me condescendingly: "Don't you know that it is New Year's Eve?"

I suppose that the eternal rhythm of the planets and the natural inclination of humans to respond to it by sleeping at night explains our universal fear of or at least healthy respect for darkness. Vision is the lord of our senses and our vision is not well developed for seeing in the dark. The Seris are no different. There are no night shifts in Seri land, no illuminated boulevards, flashing marquees or expensive street lights in Desemboque. Night remains largely a mystery and an unconquered force.

And with good reason. The desert comes alive at night. Cacti and other desert plants have evolved biological rhythms which ensure their survival. One remarkable adaptation is the special metabolic process developed by cacti that renders them biologically active in the dark. Less highly evolved plants are physiologically asleep in the darkness. So fierce is the drying power of the desert, the relentless drying force of the sun, the desicating air, the searing winds, that plants have developed novel survival strategies, including metabolic shutdown during the day. Other adaptations help— thick, waxy epidermal layers, spines replacing leaves, shallow but extensive root structures that attack every drop of moisture to penetrate the soil— these all help cactus and other desert plants to survive the perpetual drought; but more than anything else it is their nocturnal activity, including blossoming, that differentiates them from other plants.

Desert animals also tend to be nighttime creatures. In summer, only a few birds and lizards venture forth under the sun. Preserving water and maintaining a reasonable body temperature are tough chores. So why fight the sun? Come out at night when everyone else is having fun and there will be food and entertainment for all.

The Seri country abounds with snakes, more than twenty-five kinds. Especially common are three species of rattlesnakes, the sidewinder, blacktail and diamondback, while a fourth, the Mohave, makes an occasional appearance. All of them hunt at night and in great numbers in the hot months. There are also worm snakes, glossy snakes, patch-nosed snakes, spotted night snakes, shovel-nosed snakes, ground snakes, desert boas, coral snakes, gopher snakes, racers, whipsnakes, king snakes, long-nosed snakes, lyre snakes and sand snakes. And if the sea is your thing, there are highly venomous sea snakes. In addition, Seri country hosts the only poisonous lizards in the world, the Gila monster and the beaded lizard, large bulky beasts which hiss and grumble and refuse to let go if they bite.

Those who faint at the thought of snakes should not venture into the desert on a summer's night. I once camped on the desert floor on a hot evening and a small snake crawled right into my bedding. Remarkable sensation!

And there are also bugs—jejenes and mosquitos, scorpions and centipedes galore, tarantulas and kissing bugs (who transmit Chaga's disease) and blister beetles. Additionally, there must be at least ten uncatalogued species that bite or sting, for you are forever finding some new welt or bump that couldn't have come from an ordinary mosquito or gnat.

All are night beasts with which the Seris are familiar. The most feared are rattlesnakes, scorpions and centipedes, but the coyote, the mountain lion, the jaguar and the bobcat are close behind. The Seris wisely refrain from any unnecessary activity while these creatures roam.

So when darkness falls they stick to their huts. They go to sleep early. Outdoor, diurnal creatures that they are, they respond to night as do other diurnal animals. They huddle, they talk, then they sleep. So do I when I camp. Nature's rhythm and the heavy dews that fall most of the year so dictate. We who live in modern towns and cities have artificial lighting, all too much of it, to help us deny the existence of night. The Seris live under no such illusions.

Their huts are pretty dreary inside as are the houses built for them by the government. The hut was always a place to sleep, store belongings or get out of severe weather. Even today some Seris (wisely, I think) use their prefabricated government houses to store their belongings and build their own shacks for shelter. Life is an outdoors thing, except at night.

But if one can overcome the objective dangers, night is a glorious time. Dew falls heavily in all but the hottest months, a delicious cool reprieve from the parching blasts of daytime. The sky is almost always crystal clear and the view to the western horizon is unobstructed. The sounds, if you study them, are mysterious at first, then become familiar: waves, gulls, nighthawks, owls, crickets, coyotes and a myriad of unidentified insects.

The truly hazardous denizens of night, rattlesnakes and scorpions, can be avoided with minimal precautions. Fear or respect for them are legitimate. Add to these fears the stuff of mythology and creatures that go bump in the night, plus the overwhelming human instinct to stay near the night's fire and you have the basis for a lot of powerful beliefs and superstitions. Since most of us are slaves to our vision, dangers we cannot see are always more intimidating than those we can.

The only Seris I have known who have not been intimidated by night were recognized for their spiritual power. Fernando in particular was undaunted by darkness. He once walked a mile and a half to my camp in the darkness, with no flashlight, to deliver a carving. Almost everybody else, including the men, would rather not go out into the desert at night. And they don't. It's not exactly that they are afraid, it's just a lot safer not to go out. Thus there are warnings, such as, "Watch out, Daveed, the dogs will bite you," or, "There are a lot of rattlesnakes."

There is more to night, though, than meets the objectifying senses. There is more than fear of dogs, snakes, owls, coyotes and bugs. The most powerful fears the Seris harbor are for inanimate forces, dangers that lurk in the absence of light and can work their ways because the sun is not making its light available. Coyotes, as I have pointed out before, tend to visit their vengeance at night on those who have harmed or killed them. Their spirit is just one inanimate spirit that operates at night. Roberto Herrera made this clear to me one day when he described the various spirits that frequent the Seri world.

Seris fear ghosts, shades of the dead who rise from the grave to seek vengeance on those who mistreated them while they were alive. These spirits greet souls who wander at night, away from the hut and the fire, and they visit them with a sickness that no mere medical practitioner can heal. They sap the strength of those they afflict, sucking away the vital force of each victim, leaving him or her lethargic, listless, weak.

Of even greater menace, said Roberto, is an undine-like spirit, a female phantasm who derives from the sea or, sometimes, from the mountains. She is a malevolent, irascible sort, visiting unsuspecting wanderers of the night with debility and insanity, illnesses for which there are no cures. She performs such evil deeds for no apparent reason other than her general dislike of those insolent folk who venture forth by night.

As if these vapid beings were not sufficient sources of misery, there are calamities your enemies can bestow upon you by night. In the mountains near Desemboque, so Roberto's story goes, grows a cactus-like plant whose fruits auger evil for the unwary. The plant resembles a pitahaya, but the similarity is only superficial, for the fruit of this cactus, called the *cino,* carry with them the power to debilitate on contact. If you wish to bring down evil upon an enemy, the directions are simple. Take a small piece of the fruit of the cino, roll it up in a tiny scrap of cloth and attach it surreptitiously to the clothing of your intended target. The victim will experience the same symptoms as those induced by the wraith and the undine, a slow dissipation of the life force, a growing mental deterioration, and finally, disease or insanity. Fortunately, the cino is far away from the village and few are those who know its whereabouts.

Chico Romero
A storehouse of Seri lore

A cure for the disturbances brought on by these evil forces is available, but not simple. A *curandero,* or curer, must be summoned—for a fee of course—and a live caguama captured. A large bonfire is built and when it is hot, the fat from the caguama is thrown in. The fat burns, producing a thick, black smoke. The sick person must be enveloped in this smoke. The curandero then excises the bad force—usually in the form of a talisman, a doll or an insect—and screams upon seeing the form. With the shout the curandero signifies the liberation of the victim from the curse.

Not just anybody can be a curandero. Only those who have great spiritual power and many songs can aspire to curing, and often they perform with some reluctance. Hardly anyone remains nowadays who can perform the rites of healing. It seems like a lot of trouble and expense to go through when one could simply remain in one's hut at night, thus avoiding the pitfalls of mischief-makers.

Not all night forces are malevolent. Roberto attributes to older Seris the knowledge that any given midnight you can observe a benevolent spirit if you are willing to make the effort and run the risk of encountering evil forces.

Eight miles or so southwest of Desemboque, on Tepopa's flank, is a sand dune which snakes down a hill to a beach. Clearly visible from Desemboque, it is known as the *Mancha Blanca,* the White Blotch. Not far behind the Mancha Blanca is a large rock that forms a semi-cave. If you wait here, the story goes, just around midnight you will see, coming from Guardian Angel Island in the west, a spirit-whale. It will approach gliding through the waves, then soar through the air for short distances. Do not move, for it will come directly to you and at the last minute before colliding, give off a strong force which will penetrate your being with a powerful spirit, a force that will protect you from evil and harm.

Only a few have been visited by the whale, for only they have had the courage to face undaunted the unknown forces of night and await the loving sea-beast with its life-giving force. Fernando was so blessed, visited by the apparition of the spirit-whale, but he died young, only about fifty. Some evils, such as alcohol, can overcome even the gentle protection of the whale-spirit. One must work with the benevolent spirits to produce good. Alone, they are impotent.

Younger Seris don't take all this abstract stuff very seriously. Still, though, they don't run around outside at night, except to pursue a liaison or two. Younger people today do seem more beset with problems of alcoholism and drug use than did the older generation. Maybe they do run around too much at night. And maybe they don't respect the ancient forces enough.

As Seri culture is assimilated into Mexican and consumer cultures, the beauty of this kind of legendry dies. Night becomes just another natural force to be overcome, in this case with hermetically sealed homes and artificial lighting. In the Seri way, a world of often brutal but sometimes gentle powers, we see nature in the raw and the response of humanity in surprisingly candid, ancient forms, exempt from the trappings of civilization. And through the dark forces that work at night, nature balances out the good and the bad; it brings recompense to those who upset the moral equilibrium of the universe. Somehow the electric lights that are symbolic of technology bring illumination to the darkness. But they bring with them a darkness more profound than the black night they dispel.

Throughout their history the Seris have developed technology to enable them to cope with their environment. They molded the technology and used it for their own purposes—used it to strengthen their hold on life. The technology brought to them by outsiders—the trader, the government, the private companies—comes in a form that ultimately they cannot control. Their triumph over darkness will be their undoing.

Epilogue

The soil is bare now, nor can foot feel, being shod.
—Gerard Manley Hopkins

The old, wise Seris, the keepers of the lore, they who knew the old days and know the soul of the desert and the sea, are dying. There is little use for them and what they know.

Every day the noose of civilization is tightened around the throat of the ancient Seri lands. Already new subdivisions inch northward and bulldozers scrape off new lands for fields to the east. There are more shrimp boats now and fewer shrimp and the fish that eat shrimp and the fish that eat the fish that eat the shrimp are fewer also. There are too many people to feed, too many crying for land, for work. A burgeoning, poor Mexico observes hungrily that the Seri lands are mostly empty and fantasizes that in the sea lies an eternal hope. Never mind that the sea lies claimed and ravaged by a greedy humanity.

Now other Indians, poor, landless peasants from the impoverished south come northward, seeking work. They come to Kino Bay and make ironwood carvings. With electric tools they mass produce the figurines and inundate the market. They exhaust the supply of ironwood. They debase the art. The Seris watch. And imitate.

The torote is vanishing. One must spend a whole day gathering what used to be available in an hour. It is an hour's, two hours' journey to find good bushes.

Fewer Mexicans buy now. Their economy is in shambles. Only gringos buy. If the gringos do not come, the Seris cannot pay for the trucks that bring in the ironwood and torote. In Desemboque the pump that brought water to the village is broken. The government says it will fix it, but there is no money. The government owes too much to foreign banks. Farmers, increasingly impoverished themselves, haul water in by tanker. They sell it by the barrel to the Seris. But where will the money for the water come from if the gringos do not buy?

Night has visited the Seris, night with vague, amorphous powers that resist a cure. The land where the desert meets the sea is fragile, endangered, infirm. It can survive, as can its stewards, the Seri. But time is running out and the collective unconscious of the tribe is increasingly shallow, depleted, exhausted.

The People are at the edge. When they pass over, the world can expect the apocalypse.

173

Glossary

(All words are Spanish unless otherwise noted.)

Ahssah. Yes. (Seri)
Aajsh Copol Akaeet. Father of the Black Dog. (Seri)
Balsas. Small reed boats.
Bajada. Gentle alluvial slope.
Brujo. Shaman, witch.
Cabrón. Male goat; bastard (colloquial).
Caguama. Green sea turtle.
Calle Doce. 12th Street. Settlement between Hermosillo and Kino Bay.
Cantina. Bar, saloon.
Cardón cactus. Large columnar cactus (Pachycereus pringlei).
Carrizo. Cane, a reed-like plant. Also the name of an area where carrizo
    is abundant.
Casita. Shack, little house.
Chiva/chivo. Goat.
Chivero. Goatherd.
Cino. A columnar cactus that grows near Cerro Pelón and said to have
    mystical powers.
Cirio. Boojum (Fouquieria columnaris).
Comcaac. Seri name for themselves; also spelled Kunkaak. (Seri)
Contrabandistas. Smugglers.
Csipx. Lac found on creosote bushes in Seri lands. (Seri)
Curandero. Naturopathic healer.
Ejido. Communally-owned farm.

Gabachos. Outsiders.
Gringo. Yankee (in much of Latin America).
Guari. Basket made by Pima Bajo Indians. (Pima)
Infernillo. Little Hell.
Isla. Island.
Jején/jejenes. Biting gnats.
Mancha Blanca. White Spot,name of a sand dune on Tepopa Point.
Monte. Bush, toilets.
Novelas. Soap operas, sold in Mexico as books of photo dramas.
Olla. Jug, pot.
Pascola. Foot dance, performed on platform. Used by Seris, of Yaqui origin.
Panga. Small boat.
Petate. Straw mattress.
Pinche. Obscenity.
Pitahaya. Fruit of cactus (Stenocereus gummosus).
Playa. Dry lake, beach.
Santo. Talisman, image of a saint.
Sappim. Very large Seri ceremonial basket. (Seri)
Señorita. Unmarried woman.
Tinaja. Tank, collection basin, water hole.
Torote. Bush used for basket making by Seris (Jatropha cuneata).
Totuava. Sea trout.
Yori. A term for Mexicans in the Seri & Yaqui languages.

Selected Bibliography

Burkhalter, D. *The Seris.* Tucson: University of Arizona Press, 1976. A photographic essay on the Seris.

Coolidge, D. and M.R., *The Last of the Seris.* 1939. Reprint. Glorieta, New Mexico: Rio Grande Press, 1971. A literary account of a Seri shaman.

Felger, R. S. and Moser, M.B. *People of the Desert and the Sea: Ethnobotany of the Seri Indians.* Tucson: University of Arizona Press, 1985. A truly monumental work documenting the role of plants in the life of the Seri Indians.

Johnston, B. "Seri Ironwood Carving," *The Kiva*, 33 (3) 156-166, 1968. One of the earliest popular accounts of Seri ironwood carving.

McGee, W. J. *The Seri Indians.* 1898. Reprint. Glorieta. New Mexico: Rio Grande Press, 1971. A quaint account of a North American's brief encounter with the Seris.

Nabhan, Gary. *Gathering the Desert.* Tucson: University of Arizona Press, 1985. An account of the role of native plants in the diets of Indians of the Southwestern United States and Northwestern Mexico, including the Seris.

Spicer, E. H., *Cycles of Conquest.* Tucson: University of Arizona Press, 1962. A detailed history of Indians of the Southwestern United States and Northwestern Mexico, including the Seris.